Quantitative Research:

An Introduction

Third Edition

Benjamin A. Mis

Preface

Many students take an introductory class on research methods. These classes often fill students with dread because they are expected to synthesize knowledge from a large number of sources. These classes often require students to memorize facts or learn specific information and concepts, but this is done outside of a larger context. For many students who have taken a statistics class, a year later they find they can not remember the difference between a t-test and a t-shirt.

In addition, the idea of testing the natural world can seem overly complicated and beyond a single person's ability to test. Think about the information a person is bombarded with on a daily basis: commercials, commentary, and internet ads want to persuade you of something. How do you know if what you are being told is true? Aristotle believed that objects fall at a speed that is related to the weight of the object (Lloyd, 1970). Hippocrates believed that diseases were caused by an imbalance of the body's four "humors": black bile, yellow bile, blood, and phlegm (McRae, 1890). Hippocrates and Aristotle were brilliant thinkers that lived over 2300 years ago, but it took almost two thousand years for anyone to test their ideas and find out that they were wrong! If some ideas do not come naturally to you, remember that it took the human race thousands of years to figure out how to test these basic ideas about the natural world. Until recently, humans relied solely on thinking and observation when attempting to understand the natural world, and did not question ancient beliefs: it was accepted that the earth was flat, and that the sun revolved around the earth. The idea that we can make careful observations and manipulate variables to test the natural world is, historically, a recent phenomenon.

The purpose of this text is to simplify quantitative research. It is not a mystery, and it is not out of the range of the average student's ability. This text will shed light on the necessary concepts, and lead a beginning researcher step by step through the process.

References

Lloyd, G. 1970. Early Greek Science: Thales to Aristotle. New York. Norton.

McRae, C. 1890. Fathers of Biology. London. Percival & Co.

Table of Contents

Chapter 1

Introduction to Research

Topics:

1.1 Quantitative Research

The phrase "quantitative research" has been known to fill undergraduate students with terror. Yet the idea is really quite simple. Quantitative simply refers to information based on numbers. Quantitative research is research with numbers.

Why do we measure with numbers?

There are many questions about the world that can be best answered with numbers. Consider a simple question: do people who are first-generation college students perform worse in college than those that are not first-generation college students? This question, like many that you will think of, can only be meaningfully answered by using numbers. In this case, it might make sense to see if there is a difference in GPA between first-generation and non-first-generation college students.

However, not all comparisons consist of existing numbers like GPA, and the natural world is not filled with numbers. It is filled with people, animals, and things that do not have numbers. However, at a basic level, these things can be counted. For instance, counts of populations can be compared.

Even more, anything can be given a number. Numbers of siblings, age, and height are all observable variables that can be compared. It is easy to count the number of your siblings, take a look at your birth certificate, or measure your height.

The idea of quantification becomes more complicated when we consider things that are not directly observable. Take, for instance, self-esteem, intelligence, or friendliness (someone can not see or touch your IQ or self esteem or friendliness) but these things can be *quantified* and compared. Some people have high self esteem, and others have low self esteem. We know this because measures have been created that will actually let an individual measure their self esteem. Once many people have been measured, their results can be compared to others so individuals can tell whether their self esteem is high, average, or low. Another example is intelligence, which is regularly measured in IQ tests. Both self esteem and intelligence are abstract concepts that must be well defined in order to be quantified. The other example, friendliness, can be measured in the same way. How would you go about measuring how friendly someone is?

Later chapters will discuss how these things can be measured, how they can be analyzed, and how the results can be interpreted.

1.2 Interpreting the Natural World

At the beginning of recorded history, the dominant world view was that of Aristotle and Hippocrates. It was believed that reason alone could lead people to knowledge. Rene Descartes' famous statement that "I think, therefore I am" comes from this line of inquiry. This is known as *rationalism*. Rationalism states that true knowledge comes from reason alone. Many people are still rationalists, though they would not call themselves such.

The enlightenment period popularized a new kind of thinking in western civilization, called *empiricism*. Empiricism means that knowledge is acquired through the observation of the natural world, and that nothing is known through pure reason. John Locke described a newborn as a "tabula rasa" (blank slate). He thought that the child had no innate knowledge, and that everything it ever learned was through observing and interacting with the natural world.

Obviously, few people actually agree solely with either rationalism or empiricism today. These viewpoints are too extreme. Generally people accept some combination of the two. In fact, the ongoing "nature-nurture" debate stems from the argument about how much is known through reason and how much is learned from observation. The "nature" side of the argument is associated with rationalism and states that people are born with a great deal of innate knowledge. The "nurture" side of the argument is focused on experience and associated with empiricism. This side believes that people have no innate knowledge when they are born and must learn everything from their interactions with the world.

This argument takes many forms, but has powerful political ramifications. If people are blank slates when they are born, then society and how they are raised is responsible for how they behave as adults. If people are born with a great deal of innate knowledge, the environment in which they are raised is less important and therefore people, including children, bear more responsibility for their own actions and behaviors.

Modern scientific inquiry is based neither on rationalism or empiricism, but on something known as *pragmatism*. Pragmatism is a modern idea, and refers to making and testing *hypotheses* about the world. A hypothesis is a testable, falsifiable prediction. For instance, you could observe that humming birds visit your neighbors' garden but not your own. Why is this? Your neighbor jokes that the hummingbirds see the cats in your window and it scares them away. You could test this hypothesis by not letting your cats into the rooms with windows that face your garden and see if the hummingbirds come. If they do not, you could guess that hummingbirds are not coming to your garden because your neighbor has different flowers in his garden than you do. So you proceed to test the hypothesis that it is the type of flowers that the hummingbirds are attracted to, and you want to find out which flowers the birds like.

You proceed by seeing which flowers your neighbor has that you do not, and you plant Morning Glory flowers in your garden. Sure enough, humming birds visit your garden. You could stop there, or you could try other plants. You could dig up the Morning Glory and try each type of plant your neighbor has to see if more than one kind of flower is attracting the birds, as in Figure 1.

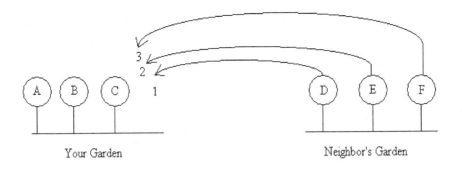

Figure 1: The systematic testing of all possibilities to find out what plants attract humming birds.

This kind of systematic investigation is what makes quantitative scientific research special. In this case, you only have flowers A, B, and C in your garden and flowers D, E and F were only in the Neighbor's garden. In order to find which of flowers D, E or F are responsible for attracting humming birds, each one must be added to your garden, one at a time. If planting flower D in your garden attracts humming birds, this tells you nothing about flowers E and F. Children tend to investigate things in a haphazard way. They might plant and tear out flowers with no clear plan. Through time, we learn that systematic investigation will give us clear answers to our questions.

Note that this hypothesis is *falsifiable*, as all hypotheses must be. For instance, if you plant flowers D, E, and F in your garden and no hummingbirds come, this means that the flowers in your neighbor's garden are not the reason (or at least not the only reason) that hummingbirds did not visit your garden. When designing a hypothesis, it is important to consider the possible outcomes.

1.3 Testable and Untestable

Not all ideas are testable. Quantitative research only allows for the examination of the observable world. It does not allow for the investigation of philosophical ideas. For instance, science can never answer the question "Is there a God," just as most religious explanations for the creation of the earth can not be supported by observation. Scientists who claim, with certainty, that there is no God are as mistaken as religious people who attempt to use religion to explain the natural world. Each question requires a different set of tools. Some questions can not be tested, and some can.

This is not meant as an attack on science or religion, only to demonstrate the difference between them. Each is very good at its job: science at explaining the observable world, and religion at explaining the meaning of life. Science can not tell us whether we have free will, but it can allow us to measure whether people think they have free will. Science can not tell us the nature of God, but it can describe for us the characteristics of creation. Science can not tell us what our purpose in life is. Religion can not tell us that the Earth is approximately 150 million kilometers from the sun.

If you can ever come up with a scientific measure that will allow you to measure whether people have free will, or answer the God question, you will be more famous than Einstein. However, the very *nature* of the question does not allow you to answer it empirically through observation! The nature of the question is about the unknown and the untestable, so no question can be devised!

Keeping these questions separate is the first step in understanding the limits and uses of quantitative research. As researchers, we will do our own jobs, and leave philosophers and theologians alone!

1.4 Logic and Arguments

Epistemology is the study of knowledge, and how we know what we think we know. All human knowledge and belief has an origin. How do you know what you know? How do you know your knowledge is correct?

Logic is important to understand in order for the researcher to devise coherent arguments. Logical arguments require evidence and consistency. Take the example of the garden and the hummingbirds. If you plant flower D in your garden and it attracts hummingbirds and then you say "flower D is completely responsible for the presence hummingbirds in the garden and flower E is not," you are making an error because you did not test flower E, so you really can not say anything about it.

Research is built on logical arguments. A researcher tests an idea because it makes sense to test that idea. You plant your neighbor's flowers in your garden to see if one of them is responsible for the hummingbirds. You can not test whether the hummingbirds just happen to like it better where your neighbor lives, because there is no specific variable you can test. If, however, you try planting flowers D, E and F in your garden and still no hummingbirds appear, then you say "I don't know why there are no birds here, but I know it is not because of the different flowers in my neighbors garden."

You will be reviewing the research of others, and each time you analyze a research study, it is important to assess the logic of the author's conclusions. It can be helpful to ask the following questions:

1. What is the author trying to study?

2. Does the author's explanation make sense?

3. Does the author's way of testing this make sense?

4. Do the results support the author's beliefs?

These explanations will become more complex as your knowledge becomes greater until you can systematically test your own ideas.

1.5 Types of Research

There are three basic types of research that will be discussed in this text. These are observational studies, experiments, and surveys.

Observational research has to do with questions about things you can see. You can ask questions about the world and the look for the answers. For instance, you can ask whether more men or women wear sandals to class in the summer. It is a simple question, and you can test it by going and observing students walking to class in the summer.

Experiments allow a researcher to measure whether the manipulation of one variable is responsible for a change in another. A researcher wants to know if raising the temperature 5 degrees in a classroom in the winter is enough to make people take their coats off. The researcher will then have two classrooms, and raise the temperature in one 5 degrees, and see if more people take their coats off in the one that is 5 degrees warmer.

Survey research allows for testing beliefs, attitudes, and behaviors by asking questions. Surveys allow for questions about the relationship between variables. A researcher can test, for instance, whether people with high self esteem also eat healthier. The researcher can devise a set of questions that will measure self esteem, and a set of questions related to healthy eating.

Each type of research, as well as the necessary statistical methods for analyzing the results obtained by the research, will be explained. Further, topics related to designing an individual research project will be discussed. This text should give you the tools necessary to begin doing your own research, and will lay out some simple step-by-step instructions for using a statistical package to analyze your results.

Often, introductory research methods and statistics tests exist separately. The purpose of studying research methods is to be able to ask well-formed questions about the natural world and to develop methods for measuring it. Statistics allow for those questions to be answered and the results interpreted. Chapter 2 will discuss the proper way to form scientific questions. Chapter 3 is about collecting data by simply making observations. Chapter 4 is the introduction to some basic topics in statistics. Chapter 5 describes how to design true experiments. Chapter 6 describes how to create a survey measure. Chapter 7 brings it all together by discussing how to create a research study and write the introduction to a research paper. Chapter 8 clarifies the difference between statistical tests, and describes when to use each one.

Key Terms:

Empiricism

Epistemology

Experiment

Falsifiable

Hypothesis

Nature-nurture

Observational research

Pragmatism

Quantified

Quantitative

Rationalism

Survey

Tabula rasa

Chapter 2

The Hypothesis: Making and Testing Assumptions

Topics:

2.1 Introduction to Testing Observations

Before starting to discuss one's own *hypothesis*, it must be clear what we are talking about. Recall that a hypothesis is a testable prediction. It is not a new conception in the annals of human history, but the dawn of modern hypothesis-based empirical science did not begin until the late sixteenth century for the western tradition. Up until that time science was mostly *deductive*. Deductive reasoning is reasoning that requires no observational input. It was believed that knowledge of the world could be divined through thought, and ancient thinkers found no reason to test their beliefs. Empirical science, the testing of predictions, and data analysis were often persecuted by the Roman Church. *Inductive* reasoning is based on observation.

Remember, then, that things we take for granted have not always been accepted, and that our modern way of thinking is fairly new in the history of humanity. Polish astronomer Nicolaus Copernicus noted that his observations of the sun, planets, and stars did not match the earth-centric universe described by Ptolemy. Ptolemy had been a Greek philosopher and astronomer and had written in the year 150. The prevailing belief was that the earth was the center of the universe, and this view was supported by the church's biblical literalism. Any other viewpoint was considered heresy, a crime punishable by death. When Copernicus' *De Revolutionibus* was published in 1543, the first printed copy was laid in his hands on the day of his death. This was a fortunate coincidence. Less fortunate was Galileo Galilei, the inventor of the telescope, who championed Copernicus' conclusions but was harassed and imprisoned for his "heretical" views during his lifetime. Galileo's heretical views included the idea that the Earth orbited the sun. Needless to say, during the late Middle Ages thinkers were beginning to test their hypothesis in order to describe the attributes of the world rather than just think about the world. Modern physics began to take shape, and scientific thinking went through a renaissance.

Another common example of deductive thought that was taken as fact was Aristotle's idea that the speed at which an object falls is dependent upon its' mass. Aristotle's scientific theories, which were formulated during the time of Alexander the Great, in the 4th century BC were taken as fact until 1586. Think about what this means. If a large heavy object like a car were pushed off of a cliff and one of the car's tires came off at the same time, the car would fall faster than the tire. In order to think about this problem, the reader should avoid the idea of drag: the shape of an object can affect the speed at which it falls because air can get caught under it. A flat piece of paper will fall more slowly than that same piece of paper crumpled up due to air molecules getting trapped under the flat sheet of paper. A skydiver relies on drag to open her parachute and slow her fall. The reader should be asking himself if Aristotle's assumption is logical, and does it match our modern view of the world.

In 1586 (in an experiment often attributed to Galileo and taking place at the Leaning Tower of Piza) the Dutch scientist Simon Stevin took balls of different sizes, climbed a church tower, and systematically dropped the balls off of the tower. Stevin found that the speed at which the balls fell was not affected by the mass of the balls. All objects fell at the same rate. It took almost two thousand years for someone to actually test Aristotle's theory.

Soon, large amounts of data, like the speed at which a body falls, began to be collected, and as empirical evidence about the nature of the world piled up scientists began to formulate new theories about our universe. A classic example is Issac Newton's development of his theory of gravitational force in the 1660's. Modern scientific thought has been around for such a short time, it is no wonder that many people have difficulty understanding the concepts of modern scientific thinking.

2.2 The Theory and the Hypothesis

A theory is a summation and explanation of a great deal of data. A theory itself is usually not testable, but it allows for testable predictions to be made about it. A theory can generate many hypotheses. Hypotheses are then used to test the assumptions of the logic of a theory. A theory is not just a consensus of opinion about someone's ideas but is a powerful collection of observations about the natural world that have been empirically tested and succinctly summarized.

For instance, amongst linguists there has been considerable debate about whether there is a critical period for second language acquisition. A critical period for language acquisition means that if a human does not begin to learn language by a certain point, that person will never be able to fully learn language. One aspect of the debate about the critical period is whether or not this theory holds true for second language acquisition. Those who support the critical period for second language acquisition argue that after a certain age, learning of a second language is universally impaired. Those who argue against this theory hold that anyone can learn a second language at any age, and therefore there is no critical period. While this debate seems to be about two different things, the theory allows for testable predictions to be made. Rarely can a single experiment change someone's mind, and so it is only through continued research that the debate can be understood and we can reach a conclusion. A hypothesis could be: "younger people who try to learn a second language will succeed better than older people who try to learn a second language". This hypothesis not only simplifies the argument, it can also be readily tested. We could measure the ability of younger people to learn a second language and compare their acquisition of that second language to a group of older people who try to learn that same second language. The theory about the critical period for language acquisition cannot directly be tested.

You can test a hypothesis, but you cannot directly test a theory; while a hypothesis focuses on one of a small number of experiments, a theory describes a large collection of data and makes predictions about how that data and other related systems might work. In general, the predictions made by a theory lead to specific hypotheses that can be tested. The data from those tests can then be incorporated into the of the world piled up scientists began to formulate new theories about our universe. A classic example is Issac Newton's development of his theory of gravitational force in the 1660's. Modern scientific thought has been around for such a short time, it is no wonder that many people have difficulty understanding the concepts of modern scientific thinking.

2.2 The Theory and the Hypothesis

A theory is a summation and explanation of a great deal of data. A theory itself is usually not testable, but it allows for testable predictions to be made about it. A theory can generate many hypotheses. Hypotheses are then used to test the assumptions of the logic of a theory. A theory is not just a consensus of opinion about someone's ideas but is a powerful collection of observations about the natural world that have been empirically tested and succinctly summarized.

For instance, amongst linguists there has been considerable debate about whether there is a critical period for second language acquisition. A critical period for language acquisition means that if a human does not begin to learn language by a certain point, that person will never be able to fully learn language. One aspect of the debate about the critical period is whether or not this theory holds true for second language acquisition. Those who support the critical period for second language acquisition argue that after a certain age, learning of a second language is universally impaired. Those who argue against this theory hold that anyone can learn a second language at any age, and therefore there is no critical period. While this debate seems to be about two different things, the theory allows for testable predictions to be made. Rarely can a single experiment change someone's mind, and so it is only through continued research that the debate can be understood and we can reach a conclusion. A hypothesis could be: "younger people who try to learn a second language will succeed better than older people who try to learn a second language". This hypothesis not only simplifies the argument, it can also be readily tested. We could measure the ability of younger people to learn a second language and compare their acquisition of that second language to a group of older people who try to learn that same second language. The theory about the critical period for language acquisition cannot directly be tested.

You can test a hypothesis, but you cannot directly test a theory; while a hypothesis focuses on one of a small number of experiments, a theory describes a large collection of data and makes predictions about how that data and other related systems might work. In general, the predictions made by a theory lead to specific hypotheses that can be tested. The data from those tests can then be incorporated into the theory in order to improve the theory. This repetitive cycle of test→improve theory→test→improve theory, etc. leads to robust theories that are well supported by the evidence.

2.3 Formulating a Technical Hypothesis

Consider what you have learned about the *scientific method*. This is probably not a new idea to you. The scientific method is a basic set of steps for studying a topic. It can be stated in different ways, but generally looks like this:

1. Ask a question

2. Make observations

3. Formulate hypothesis

4. Test hypothesis

5. Analyze data

6. Draw conclusions

7. Communicate results

Refine Hypothesis

Note that the scientific method does not have to end with one run through the steps. Each time, the hypothesis can be refined and steps 4-7 can be repeated.

Good quantitative research starts with an intelligent question about the observable world. After observations are made, including background research, a hypothesis is formed. The definition of the hypothesis is now going to be stated in more technical terms: a hypothesis is a statement about the relationship between two variables. For instance, the second language study mentioned earlier is a correlational study. The hypothesis states that "as age increases, performance on a grammaticality task decreases". The hypothesis is about the relationship between variables. In this case, the hypothesis states that as one variable, age, increases, the other variable, performance, decreases. This is a negative relationship, and negative in this case, only describes the direction of the relationship. Figure 1 is a graph of hypothetical data from a study of second language acquisition as a function of age.

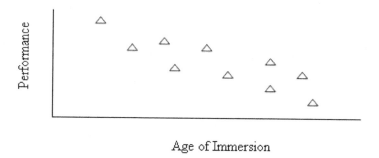

Figure 2.1: As age increases, performance decreases. This relationship is described in a scatter-plot, where each data point on the graph denotes one person tested.

In order to clarify the relationship in the data, a line is often added which shows the general trend (Figure 2). The negative relationship, as seen in this example is the line that runs from the upper left to the lower right. A positive relationship would run in the other direction, and in a case where there is no relationship between the two variables, there would be no line that would fit the graph well.

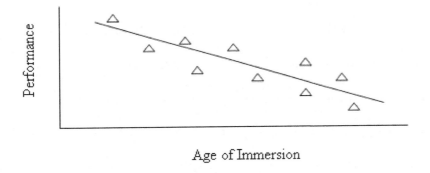

Figure 2.2: The data used in Figure 1 with a regression line included to highlight the hypothetical relationship.

To formulate this hypothesis technically, it is important to be able to state the hypothesis. To do this, two hypotheses must be stated. These are called the experimental hypothesis, (or H1) and the null hypothesis (or H0). In the second language example, if you recall, the experimental hypothesis is:

H1: As age increases, performance on a grammaticality task decreases.

The null hypothesis is:

H0: As age increases, performance on a grammaticality task does not decrease.

The null hypothesis is the complement of the experimental hypothesis. We state both the experimental hypothesis and the null hypothesis because the statistical tests that you will do actually test the null hypothesis, not the experimental hypothesis. The relationship between the experimental hypothesis, the null hypothesis, and statistical testing will be explained fully in Section 3.3. Often, the null hypothesis will be stated first because it is a statement of no difference, or equality. However, since we are actually working with the experimental hypothesis, that will be our starting point.

In the example in Figure 2.1 and Figure 2.2, we are working with *variables*. A variable is whatever you are measuring: in the second language acquisition example, the variables are *age of immersion* and *performance*. There are three ways of describing the relationship between variables. For this example, lets propose the following study: fifty students take a test, and you want to compare the results of these students to the general population. You could hypothesize that:

(1) H1: These students will perform **better** than the general population.

      students>population

H0: These students will **not** perform **better** than the general population.

      students≤population

(2) H1: These students will perform **worse** than the general population.

      students<population

H0: These students will **not** perform **worse** than the general population.

      students≥population

(3) H1: These students will perform **differently** than the general population.

      students≠population

H0: These students will **not** perform **differently** than the general population.

      students=population

Notice the way the null and experimental hypotheses are written. The mathematical statement below each population shows how the two groups will be related. The null provides the complement of the experimental hypothesis. Figure 2.3 presents the relationship between H1 and H0.

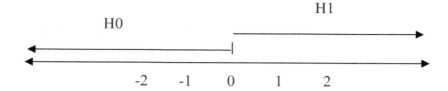

Figure 2.3: Difference between students and population, with H1 students>population and H0 students≤population. The lines below H1 and H0 show the hypothesized difference (students score minus population score) under the two hypotheses. Note that H0 contains zero, which represents no difference between the groups.

Time to work: Draw the relationship between H1 and H0 for (2) and (3) to demonstrate your understanding of how these variables relate to each other.

2.4 Relationships Between Variables

It is important to identify the variables in the hypothesis. In this study, Age is measurable, and so is performance. The prediction is that a change in age produces a change in performance. The hypothesis in (4) makes the statement mathematical by replacing age with 'x' and performance with 'y'.

(4) A change in x produces a change in y.

The variables x and y can now be replaced by any variables that have this type of relationship, as seen in Table 2.1.

Table 2.1. Variables with a measurable relationship.

x-variable	y-variable
study time	grades
alcohol consumption	ability to drive
driving speed	the likelihood of receiving a ticket
sunlight exposure	plant health

The list could easily continue. Note that the generalized hypothesis (4) does not make a prediction about the direction of the relationship, while the hypothesis "as age increases, performance on a grammaticality task decreases" does make a prediction about direction. The generalized hypotheses, described below, predict directionality.

(5) An increase in x produces an increase in y.

(6) An increase in x produces a decrease in y.

There will be rare cases when the inverse hypotheses 2 and 3 will not be true, but those need not be noted. For our purposes, (7) has the same meaning as (5) and (8) the same meaning as (6).

(7) A decrease in x produces a decrease in y.

(8) A decrease in x produces in increase in y.

In all studies, the variables x and y must be measurable in order for meaningful data to be collected. Note that causality is not always assumed by a hypothesis. A causal hypothesis requires an experimental manipulation (more is explained about the experimental manipulation in Chapter 5). If the researcher is not responsible for the experimental manipulation, causation cannot be assumed. Examples (2) through (5) are causal hypotheses because they predict that the change in variable x is responsible for the change in variable y. A non-causal hypothesis is simply making a statement about the state of the world and is often called a correlational hypothesis. For instance, the hypothesis "an increase in neighborhood diversity is related to a decrease in prejudice" does not state that the multi-racial area causes a reduction in prejudice, only that increased diversity is related to a decrease in prejudice. Hypotheses (9) and (10) are examples of a correlation hypothesis.

(9) An increase in x is related to an increase in y.

(10) An increase in x is related to a decrease in y.

In order to test this hypothesis, data must be gathered on the diversity of various neighborhoods and we must measure the levels of prejudice in the residents of those neighborhoods. Causation cannot be predicted in this type of study. Why? It could be true that when someone is exposed to a variety of races and ethnicities, a person is less prejudiced, and that living in a diverse neighborhood makes people less prejudiced. It might also be true, however, that people who choose to live in diverse neighborhoods are less prejudiced to begin with!

How could this study be made experimental? A researcher must randomly select people to live in different neighborhoods, and this would be difficult. A researcher might get a college campus to allow him to randomly assign students to different dorms with different levels of diversity, and then measure the prejudice levels of the students after 6-months in their new environment. Random-assignment means that each student in the study has an equal chance of being in the diverse dorm or the non-diverse dorm. If causation is shown, the words in (9) and (10) "is related to" can be replaced with "causes." In this study, the results of our manipulation might support a causal hypothesis because the researcher is assigning people to groups randomly. Random-assignment allows the researcher gets to assume that the groups are equivalent at the beginning, and any measurable effect is therefore the result of the experimental manipulation.

Time to work: why is it better to have 2 groups, than to simply measure the group in the diverse dorm before and after? Why do you only have to measure the difference between the two groups once?

2.5 Conceptual, Operational, Measurable

The process of developing a workable research plan first requires the development of a hypothesis. However, when dealing with abstract concepts, there are a few steps involved in developing the hypothesis. In order to develop a conceptual or operational hypothesis, we first go through the processes of *conceptualization* and *operationalization*. By conceptualization, we mean the we clearly define our concepts, and this is particularly important when we are dealing with abstract concepts. A *conceptual hypothesis* provides you with meaning. It is usually a clear definition of the concepts you wish to measure. By operationalization, we are talking about the ways we plan to observe those constructs. You can not say how you will observe your construct, however, until you clearly define that construct. An *operational hypothesis*, which takes those concepts and describes ways we can observe those concepts in the real world. The measures will be the tools you use to actually collect data, and are often developed later in the experimental design process. If you do a poor job of developing conceptual and operational definitions, however, your measures may not actually be measuring what you want to measure, and you will be left with results that do not make sense.

If measuring abstract concepts like "love" or "happiness" strikes you as strange, you are not alone. I had a discussion about what makes people happy with a very intelligent professor of literature, who argued, with good merit, that the concept of "happiness" is unmeasurable because it is subjective. He had a good point. Each person's idea of happiness means something different to them, so it is impossible to compare people's individual levels of happiness to each other in some objective way. Yet we can compare how different people rate their level of happiness, but it requires a more complex design than simply asking "are you happy?" This is where our quantitative methods are really put to use. The very first thing we have to do is define "happiness." We all know what it means to be happy, but writing out that clear definition is imperative in designing a study to measure "happiness." This requires us to do some work. Go ahead and write down your definition of "happiness." Now, it is important to consider concepts that are similar to "happiness." Is your definition of happiness different from your definition of "life satisfaction" or "optimism?" Think about what makes each of these concepts different. If your concept of "happiness," for instance, overlaps with your concept of "optimism," you might not really be measuring "happiness." Any results you find relating to happiness might actually be relating to "optimism," because you did not carefully define what makes the concept of "happiness" special compared to other concepts. Doing this is not easy, but turning abstract concepts into measurable constructs is one of the great goals of this kind of research. Becoming good at this kind of analysis will help you to see the world in a clearer, more precise way.

In fact, if we are clear and precise in our designs, we have taken a huge step forward in performing good quantitative research. Many clever research projects were derailed after a lot of hard work was completed because the researcher did a poor job defining the concepts he or she was studying. This does not mean you have to reinvent the wheel each time you perform a study: use the resources already available by looking at how other researchers defined the concepts you want to study. Maybe you can borrow from them (with the appropriate citation, of course), or maybe you could even improve on their conceptualizations. Once we have a clear definition, we can move on to describing ways we can observe our concepts. Never try to measure a concept, though, before you have good conceptual and operational definitions.

Lets consider how we could develop a way to measure "intelligence". Start with the conceptualization: how might you define "intelligence?" It might be a combination of "knowledge and experience leading to an ability to solve problems" (of course, we must then define knowledge and experience to have a good hypothesis). Webster's Dictionary defines intelligence as "the ability to learn or understand or deal with new or trying situations." We could start with that definition. What can be done with that definition to make it operational, to make it scientifically testable? Can you test "the ability to learn or understand or deal with new or trying situations?" In a conceptual definition, a concept is usually defined in terms of other concepts, which are often also difficult to measure. Assume that a researcher would like to measure the difference in intelligence between two groups. In order to develop her hypothesis, a clear definition is required.

Intelligence cannot be measured by observing a person in a natural setting. What would we look at to get a measure of intelligence? It must be defined in some other way. The process of operationalization is the process of defining the concept in a way that allows us to observe the concept. If I asked you to measure intelligence, you might suggest we use an IQ test. This would be reasonable. Just remember that an IQ test is the measure itself, not the operationalization. The operationalization is the way in which an IQ test measures intelligence: by observing your knowledge, comprehension, and problems solving ability. Be careful to not confuse the measure with the operationalization. The measure is far more specific, in this case, the many questions of the IQ test. You can see how the three parts of developing measures interact in Table 2.2.

Table 2.2: The process of conceptualization, operationalization and measuring intelligence

Conceptualization	Operationalization	Measure
ability to learn ⟶	how much knowledge someone has ⟶	questions that measure knowledge
ability to understand ⟶	how well they comprehend new information ⟶	questions that measure comprehension
ability to deal with new or trying ⟶ situations	how well they solve problems ⟶	complex problems to solve

As you can see in Table 2.2, the concept of "intelligence" is broken down into parts, and each of those parts is linked to an operationalization, which in turn is linked to a measure. This does not have to be a one-to-one relationship: you can have multiple operationalizations for a single measure, and multiple questions for a single operationalization.

Now, we can put the parts together into a hypothesis:

H1: Children who go through an early learning program will have more ability to learn or understand or deal with new or trying situations than those who do not go through a head-start program.

H0: People who go through a head-start program will not be more intelligent than those who do not go through a head-start program.

This hypothesis is stating that intelligence can actually be affected by participation in a program. Note that intelligence is a construct, but attending a head-start program is not. Attending a head-start program is not a construct; it is already directly observable. As has already been discussed, intelligence can be measured on an IQ test. Children may be randomly assigned to the program, and then their IQs can be measured. The measure itself is simply the list of questions that make up the IQ test.

Therefore, our operational hypothesis is:

H1: People who go through a head-start program will have more knowledge, a better comprehension ability, and a better problem solving ability than those who do not go through a head-start program.

H0: People who go through a head-start program will not have more knowledge, a better comprehension ability, and a better problem solving ability than those who do not go through a head-start program.

A note about ethics: consider the ethical implications of assigning some children to a head-start program and not assigning others to the same program. Do children benefit so much from a program that it is wrong to not allow them all to go the program?

Summary of Research:

The hypothesis makes a measurable prediction. The conceptual hypothesis is the general, abstract hypothesis. The operational hypothesis is observable. When a hypothesis is formed, it is important to know what the data will look like. The researcher must know what the variables are and how they will be measured. In general a hypothesis is more useful if it makes a causal prediction.

Key Terms

Causal Hypothesis

Conceptualization

Conceptual Hypothesis

Correlational Hypothesis

Deductive

Experimental Hypothesis

Hypothesis

Inductive

Null Hypothesis

Operationalization

Operational Hypothesis

Scientific Method

Variable

Problems

1) For each of the following problems, indicate: What are the variables? What is the independent variable and the dependent variable?

a) An increase in smoking causes an increase in cancer risk.

b) The speed at which an object falls is affected by the weight of the object.

c) The speed at which an object falls is affected by the shape of the object.

d) Drug A will help bald people grow hair better than drug B.

2) Define "happiness" conceptually and operationally, and suggest a few questions for how it could be measured.

3) Formulate a hypothesis to test the following ideas, and explain how your hypothesis could be tested. Be specific about how you would design the study and what measures you would use:

a) John thinks that people who are more religious do better in school.

b) Do people think the death penalty is justified more or less based on the crime that has been committed?

Chapter 3

Observation of Human Systems

Topics:

3.1 Introductory Problem

When attempting to describe cultural phenomena (measuring human interactions), there is a great deal of data that can be easily collected. You can ask about what people are wearing, what they are doing or what they are planning to do; when we record these observations we are describing the appearance of things. Most people make judgments based on appearance every day. In this section, you will learn how to make systematic observations of human behavior using quantitative methods.

Take a very simple example: people drink coffee. Premium coffee houses are very popular, and many people don't think twice about spending five dollars on a cup of some fancy java drink. Do you think that executives at the big coffee firms do research to determine who is buying their coffee and who is not? Sales data is good, solid information that can help them expand their business and subsequently make more money.

How can they do this?

That question will be answered using the following example. This type of data is easy to collect, easy to analyze and can tell you a lot about a business. This chapter will introduce you to a simple approach for gathering the type of data that can answer real world questions.

Consider two competing coffeehouses in a small town: John's Java and Rachel's Roast. They both sell a lot of coffee. They are both on the same street. Rachel, the owner of Rachel's roast, drives by John's Java every day and thinks that a lot of young business people are purchasing their coffee there, while her clientele consists primarily of college students and families. Rachel thinks that she is losing out on a lot of customers and that she could make more money if she was getting some of those customers from John, but before she commits money to an advertising campaign and makes changes to her coffee shop, she wants to be sure that what she is seeing is a real statistical difference between the clientele at her shop and the customers at John's Java.

Assume that you are the assistant manager at Rachel's Roast, and she assigns you the task of figuring out whether she is losing out on the young business crowd. You start with the following hypothesis: more of the young business crowd is going to John's Java than Rachel's Roast.

H1: Rachel and John have a different proportion of business and non-business customers.

H0: Rachel and John do not have a different proportion of business and non business customers.

First, you must define young business people. You do not want to accidentally count a well dressed college student as a business person or a laid back business person as a college student. So to define "business person", you assign a set of characteristics: they arrive at the coffeehouse before 9AM and leave quickly. Men are dressed in either a button down or polo shirt and women are dressed in a blouse and skirt, a dress, or a suit. Are these categories perfect? How could you fix them?

It would be possible to just go and count the number of young business people at Rachel's and at John's but John's is a little busier because it is in a busier location, so just counting the number of young business people won't work. If you did that and did not consider overall proportions, it might be true that John has more business people, but it would not let Rachel know whether this was due to a different distribution of types of customers or if this is due to John's Java being a busier coffee house. The answer is to collect the total number of business and non-business customers at both John's and Rachel's and then compare the results.

The tally sheet might look something like this:

	John's Java	Rachel's Roast
Business Customer	A	B
Non-Business Customer	C	D

Each row and column is labeled. This is a 2X2 *contingency table* because you are collecting information on two types of customers from two locations. A contingency table is used to record the relationship between two (or more) categorical variables. The first 2 is the number of rows, and the second 2 is the number of columns. You could imagine a 2X3, 3X3, or any size table. Box A will be a count of business customers at John's Java, and box C will be the count of non-business customers at John's Java. Boxes B and D will record the same counts for Rachel's Roast. This way, a simple statistical analysis will show whether John's Java or Rachel's Roast has more business customers compared to the number of other customers, and consequently whether Rachel should invest in attracting those customers.

There some other concerns we should address before the study is started: a strategy has to be worked out for situations when the person counting is not sure whether the person being counted is a business customer or a non-business customer. Perhaps you could assign the not-sures to the non-business boxes. Sometimes people have different ideas of what "business" or "non-business" is, so the difference in the not sure column could be a problem. The easiest way to solve this problem is to have one person do all the data collection. However, for two locations, this is impossible, and it is also possible that some days might be busier than others, or some weeks might be busier than others.

The next step, then, is to effectively operationalize the measure. The concepts being measured are business and non-business customers. What does that mean, exactly? As noted, if each person used their own idea of what business and non-business customers look like, you may end up comparing two measures that are actually quite different.

Time to work: how will you classify business and non-business customers? How will you know the difference? Clearly define what you are looking for in each, as if you were giving instructions to two people who will be doing the counting.

Now it is time to go about collecting data. It is important to have a plan for that, too. Maybe Monday's are really busy, and more business customers get coffee on Monday, so if you compare Rachel's Roast on Monday with John's Java on Tuesday you will get data that is biased, just as if you had one person who said "not-sure" a lot to Rachel's customers and a person who said "non-sure" to a few of John's customers. These kinds of problems could change the outcome of your study. However, in all research there will always be these kinds of additional variables to consider. The best way to deal with these types of uncertainties is to control for them as well as you can.

How much data do you need? It could be easiest to start with a brief study to see if there is any noticeable difference between the two coffee shops. If there appears to be a real difference, then more data could be collected.

3.2 The Research Plan

You assign Sara to collect data from John's Java and Javier to collect data from Rachel's Roast, both on Tuesday. You then switch them and have Sara collect data from Rachel's and Javier collect data from John's on Wednesday. After 2 days of data gathering by Sara and Javier, your tally sheet looks like this:

	John's Java	Rachel's Roast
Business Customer	A 53	B 22
Non-Business Customer	C 29	D 44

The number in each box represents the number of customers in that category. Box A, for instance, is the total number of business customers observed entering John's Java.

One might suggest that we only have to count business customers, since Rachel wants to see who has more business customers. Then, Rachel would just compare the 531 customers that John had with the 227 customers that she had and conclude that John's Java has more business customers than Rachel's Roast.

However, to conclude that this difference is statistically significant we would perform a Chi-Square test. Simply add A+C, B+D, A+B, and C+D to get the row and column totals, which we use to calculate the expected values. Also, add A+B+C+D together to get the total number of observations. Now most of the calculations necessary for the chi-square statistic have been completed.

	John's Java	Rachel's Roast	Totals
Business Customer	A 53	B 22	75
Non-Business Customer	C 29	D 44	73
Totals	82	66	148

So over the course of 2 days, John's served 82 people and Rachel served 66 people for a total of 148 customers between the two coffee shops. Over half (51%) of the customers who frequented the coffee shops were business customers. It also appears that there is a difference in the number of business customers served by the two shops. A larger portion of John's business is "Business Persons" (65%), while Rachel's customers are mostly non-business (67%). Are these proportions statistically significant?

This next section is about the statistical analysis of the 2X2 contingency table. It will be discussed here instead of in the statistics chapters because it is relatively simple mathematically. Also, this chapter alone will provide you with all of the tools necessary to perform an observation study and compare statistical differences in rates.

There are two variables in the java table, each with 2 levels. The first variable is business or non-business, and the second variable is John's or Rachel's. The appropriate test to use here is called a chi-square test for independence. There are many calculators that will do the math for you, but for a 2X2 case the math is fairly simple.

The formula is:

$$\chi^2 = \frac{(ad-bc)^2\,(a+b+c+d)}{(a+b)(c+d)(a+c)(b+d)}$$

So to calculate the coffeehouse statistics, plug in the numbers from the tally sheet into the formula.

$$\chi^2 = \frac{[(53*44)-(22*29)]^2(53+22+29+44)}{(53+22)(29+44)(53+29)(22+44)}$$

$$\chi^2 = \frac{(2332-638)^2(148)}{75*73*82*66}$$

$$\chi^2 = 14.33$$

The example above demonstrates how to calculate the chi-square for a 2X2 contingency table. Many statistical packages will perform that calculation for a 2X2 contingency table as well as more complicated situations with more rows and columns. The next step is to look up this value in a table to see if it is statistically significant, but first, the degrees of freedom must be calculated. For a chi-square table of any size, the formula for the degrees of freedom is:

$$(rows-1)*(columns-1)$$

Since this is a 2X2 table, the number of degrees of freedom is 1. Look up the chi-square *critical value* of 14.33 with 1 degree of freedom. Look up the critical value at the .05 level. As you will find, a chi-square with 1 degree of freedom and a p value of .05, must be equal to or greater than 3.841. That means that any value greater than 3.841 is *statistically significant*, the likelihood of us observing a chi-square value of 14.33 by chance is less than .05. In this case, the result of the chi-square test suggests that there is a real difference between the proportion of business customers at John's and Rachel's. Now Rachel has statistical evidence that suggests that her initial assumption was correct.

3.3 P-value and the Null Hypothesis

The p-value must be understood in the context of the null hypothesis before it can be interpreted. The p-value is a probability, but not a probability that you are right or wrong. All statistical tests are tests of the null hypothesis. The null hypothesis is the complement of your hypothesis. If Rachel's hypothesis is that there is a difference in the clientele between her store and John's store, then the null hypothesis is that there is not a difference in the clientele between her store and John's store. If Rachel's hypothesis is that John gets more business customers than she does, the null hypothesis is that either John gets less business customers than Rachel, or there is no difference. The null hypothesis is that you are wrong, that nothing is happening, or that there is no difference between your groups. Then, when you run a statistical test, you will be given a p-value in your statistical output.

The p-value is the probability of the data being produced by random chance if the null is true.

The p-value can be between 0 and 1. A large p-value means that there is a high probably of the data being produced by chance. Normally, you do not want the null hypothesis to be true, so the smaller the probability that the null hypothesis is true, the better. Most often, researchers set something called the alpha before they start a test. The alpha is the level at which a researcher accepts their results as supporting their hypothesis. An alpha of 0.05, for instance, means that you are willing to accept a 5% chance that your results were produced by chance, and you will have to find a p-value less than alpha, or 0.05, in order to assume that your results differ from chance. The smaller the p-value, the more likely your results really do reflect reality and were not observed by chance. Finding a p-value of 0.05, for instance, still means that that even if the null hypothesis is true, you will still get results as extreme or more extreme as the results you found one time for every 20 times you conduct your study. This is the reason a smaller p-value means you are more likely to have found an effect. It is important to note that a p-value of 0.05 means there is a 5% chance that the data was produced by chance. Most researchers are comfortable with this, and are willing to set alpha to 0.05 and say that a p-value of less than alpha, or 0.05, shows that a significant effect was observed.

This example demonstrates how easy and useful statistical testing can be, and what it can show. It may have been clear earlier that there was a big difference in the proportions between business customers at Rachel's and at John's. The diagonal is the part to look at here. If $(ad-bc)^2$ is going to be a large value, there is a good chance there will be a statistical difference. If $(ad-bc)^2$ is small, there might not be a statistical difference.

Sometimes the outcome is not at all clear. It is possible to observe a difference, but have that difference be the product of random chance and not be a statistical difference. Suppose you have less data and the table looks like this:

	John's Java	Rachel's Roast	Totals
Business Customer	A 8	B 4	12
Non-Business Customer	C 3	D 5	8
Totals	11	9	20

It might also look like there is a large difference, since John has twice as many business customers as Rachel, and Rachel has almost twice as many non-business customers as John. There is a problem with this conclusion but to show the problem we can not even use a chi-square test. The chi-square test will not work! There are some basic requirements that the data must meet in order to run a chi-square test. One requirement is that the minimum expected number of observations per cell is 5. Although this precludes the use of the chi-square, this is not a big problem, because there is another test called the Fisher's Exact Test that will allow you to determine if this difference is real when your sample size is small. Unfortunately, Fisher's Exact test is not as powerful as the chi-square test. A less powerful test might not pick up on statistical differences that are real but small.

In addition to the exact test, Ronald Fisher was responsible for the F-test. He was a brilliant statistician and almost single handedly created the field of statistics. His strong support for the study of evolution led to an unfortunate involvement in the study of eugenics, which may have tarnished his legacy, but his contributions to statistics cannot be ignored. Fisher was British, so he knew a lot of people who drank tea with milk. Particularly, he knew a woman named Ms. Bristol who reported that she could tell whether milk or tea was put in the cup first. Fisher thought this to be a ridiculous notion, and subsequently developed a method for testing her ability.

Consider the following table:

	Said tea first	Said milk first	Totals
Tea first	A 8	B 4	12
Milk first	C 3	D 5	8
Totals	11	9	20

Fisher then systematically tested Ms. Bristol to see if she could tell the difference between cups that had tea added first and cups that had milk added first. These are the same numbers as the table above, but now the headings have been changed: for instance, the number in box A represents the cases where tea was added to the cup first, and Ms. Bristol said that tea was added first. At first glance, it appears that Ms. Bristol may have some skill at determining the order in which the tea and milk were added to the cup. Before making this assumption, though, Fisher's exact test will tell us whether this data represents a significant difference or is merely a product of chance.

$$p=\frac{(A+B)!(C+D)!(A+C)!(B+D)!}{(A+B+C+D)!A!B!C!D!}$$

$$p=\frac{12!*8!*11!*9!}{20!*8!*4!*3!*5!}$$

$$p=.165$$

Fisher's Exact Test takes into account of all possible combinations of the numbers in the contingency tables, and returns the probability that the results you found support the null hypothesis. Since the probability that the null hypothesis is true is greater than .05, we must assume that these data are a product of chance! Since .165 is greater than .05, the calculations stop here; in order to calculate the actual p-value, this p-value must be added to the most extreme possible combinations of values:

```
add
8  4
3  5
with
9  3
2  6
and
10  2
1   7
and
11  1
0   8
```

The calculations must be repeated for each of those 2X2 table. Then, the probabilities of each possible combination of outcomes is combined. There are a number of statistical packages that will perform the calculation for you much more quickly than can be accomplished by hand.

Now, look back at this table:

	John's Java	Rachel's Roast	Totals
Business Customer	A 8	B 4	12
Non-Business Customer	C 3	D 5	8
Totals	11	9	20

It still appears that there is a difference, but when we run Fisher's Exact Test, we find that the p-value is .362. This means that the probability of finding results this extreme, or more extreme, are expected to happen 36.2% of the time if the data are being produced by chance. Another note is that small sample sizes can be a problem. If data is being generated by chance, it is much more likely to get results like this:

	John's Java	Rachel's Roast
Business Customer	8	4
Non-Business Customer	3	5

than to get results like this:

	John's Java	Rachel's Roast
Business Customer	800	400
Non-Business Customer	300	500

Notice that each value has now been multiplied by a factor of 100. When we do a chi-square with this data, we get a p-value that is very small, less than .001. It is common to get values that *appear* to be extreme in a smaller sample. The statistical tests allow us to see whether those numbers that appear to be extreme are actually *statistically significant*!

In addition to the 2X2 chi-square test used in this chapter, a chi-square test can be performed on a matrix of any size. For example, some students might want to ask how students arrived on campus. They might ask if more students arrived by car or by bus, and they might hypothesize that more women would drive or get rides and more men would ride the bus because men would be more comfortable with public transportation. They watched students arrive where there was a bus stop near a parking lot and drop-off area. Here are their results:

	Bus	Car
Male	A	B
Female	C	D

This 2X2 matrix allows for a comparison between two modes of transportation. While gathering their data they observe that a lot of students arrive on campus by bicycle. We can add this outcome to our tally sheet to create a 2X3 data matrix.

	Bus	Car	Bicycle
Male	A	B	E
Female	C	D	F

Now a comparison can be made between three methods of transportation. The mathematics behind these larger matrices is more complicated, but most statistical packages can easily analyze this data for you. A significant chi-square value, however, will bring some interpretive difficulties. A significant value will tell you that there is a difference, but it will not tell you where the difference lies. Do more men than women ride the bus compared to driving, or is the significant difference in the comparison between taking a car and riding a bicycle? In order to fully investigate the area of difference, three matrices can be made from the above matrix. This includes the original comparison of bus and car, but also bus-bicycle and car-bicycle.

	Bus	Bicycle
Male	A	E
Female	C	F

	Car	Bicycle
Male	B	E
Female	D	F

As the complexity of a design increases, so does the complexity of the analysis.

3.4 Problems in Observation

Two possible problems encountered in observation studies are the Hawthorne Effect and the Pygmalion Effect. The Hawthorne Effect was observed in the Hawthorne Electric factory in the 1930's when researchers became interested in ways to scientifically increase production. Researchers went into the factory and observed people working and made various changes to see if they could increase production. They adjusted lighting, break times, lunch times, and anything else they thought might make a difference in performance. Everything they did, however, led to an increase in production! When they undid a change, this also increased production! They knew that this could not be the result of the manipulations alone, and the researchers came to the conclusion that it was the observations themselves that led to the increase in production. All future researchers benefit from their rather common sense observation: when people are being observed by researchers, they do not behave the same way they do when they are not being observed. This behavior is known as the *demand characteristic*. The demand characteristic occurs when a participant in a study forms an idea of what the researcher is looking for and modifies their behavior accordingly.

The Pygmalion Effect is based on the idea of teacher expectation. Think of the brilliant "blue eyes-brown eyes" demonstration by Jane Elliot, where she separated young children into dominant and oppressed groups so they could experience racism and prejudice in a small, non-racially diverse community. One important finding in her study was that students actually performed worse on tests when they were in the oppressed group. The oppressed group was told that they were not as "good" and "smart" as the dominant group. The students actually performed more poorly on tests when they were in the oppressed group, leading to the conclusion that people will perform to expectations! In addition, it should be noted that the researcher's expectations will lead to bias in observations, even if the researcher is on guard. This is the reason for double-blind studies, when neither the researcher nor the subject knows which group the subject is in so that objective observations can be made.

Key Terms:

alpha

Chi-square (χ^2)

Contingency table

Critical value

Demand characteristic

Fisher's Exact Test

Hawthorne Effect

Null hypothesis

P-value

Pygmalion Effect

Statistically significant

Problems

1) You look at the proportions of men and women in different majors. You find there are 225 men and 355 women in the Sociology program, and 230 men and 520 women in the Engineering program. Is there a difference in proportion? What is the chi-square and p-value?

2) Design a study to compare whether men or women on your campus are more likely to carry backpacks.

    a)Create a table to collect data

    b)Decide where and when you will collect data

References

Bulfinch, T. 1913. Age of Fable: Vols. I & II: Stories of Gods and Heroes.

DeLisa, J.; Gans, B.; Walsh, N. 2005. Physical medicine and rehabilitation: principles and practice, Volume 1, Lippincott Williams & Wilkins.

Howell, D. 2009. Statistical Methods for Psychology. Cengage Learning.

Miller, F.; Vandome, A.; McBrewster, J. 2010. The Hawthorne Effect. VDM Publishing House

Chapter 4

Introduction to Statistics

Topics:

4.1 Overview of Descriptive Statistics

4.2 Standard Deviation and Variance

4.3 Types of Variables

4.1 Overview of Descriptive Statistics

Numbers are everywhere. For humans, they hold meaning. The numbers on the clock and the calendar mark the passage of time. Ask a child how old they are and they will tell you how many years they have been alive. The numbers on your bank account statement mark the amount of money you have available. Even things that we don't regularly think of as numbers allow for a simple conversion. There is a needle on your dash board that lets you know how much gas you have in your tank. Usually, this is a proportion. How much do you have? A half tank? A quarter? A half tank is .5 of a tank, a quarter tank is .25 of a tank.

We use numbers to mark things, to make life easier. How many days are left until Spring break, Christmas vacation, or your next test?

Do you have enough money to pay the rent? You know the answers to these questions because you know where to find the answers. Using statistical methods to see if there is a relationship between two variables is not much different. Yet many people find the numbers intimidating. The stats in this chapter only require you to be able to add, subtract, multiply, and divide. The purpose of these chapters is to start you on your way to real research and statistical analysis by focusing on just a few easy to use methods. There is no hazing or complicated password to master that will allow you entry into the ranks of researchers who understand data. These are all simple calculations that only require you to take the time to perform them. Understanding data is far simpler when you understand how some simple statistics are generated.

This chapter is about descriptive statistics for many reasons. They are easy to understand, easy to use, and are also very useful. Descriptive statistics allow for a simple and fast summary of data, especially when your data consists of a large number of observations. Data simply refers to information. A *data set* is a collection of pieces of information. Every data set tells a story, and the first part of understanding that story is to describe what is there. We will start working with some real numbers.

This data set is a collection of the ages of students in a research class:

23	22	21	33
21	23	22	21
24	23	23	23
23	22	22	27
25	24	21	20
24	24	22	24
25	22	23	30

So far these are just a bunch of numbers. But they can yield a lot of useful data. Sets of numbers are called *distributions*. A distribution is just a collection of values that come from some kind of measurement. These are the real ages of students in an upper division research methods course. So far this is just a list of numbers. There is real information here. What can we do with this information?

Start with calculating the average age of the class. What is the average age of these students? You can discover this by adding together all of the ages and then dividing that sum by the number of students in the class. The number of students, in this case, is the number of observations. From now on, the number of observations will be written as "n".

Total ages:	676
Number of students:	29
Average:	23.31

Another name for the average is the *mean*. Mean is just a technical term. Now, what is the *median* of the numbers? You can calculate that by just ordering the numbers from highest to lowest and finding the one in the middle. The median tells us what the midpoint is of all the observations.

Median: 23

Another descriptive number is the *mode*. The mode is the most frequently occurring observation. You can calculate this by looking for the most common number. You can see this by looking at the histogram in Figure 1. Each bar represents the number of observations for each age group. Whichever bar is the highest is the mode.

Mode: 23

A histogram is one way of presenting data, and is particularly useful when you have many observations and you want to show which observations are the most common and which observations are the least common. A histogram allows you to see the distribution, or pattern, of the data. In this case, we are able to take the list of numbers above and graphically represent it in a way in which relationships between the numbers are clear. It is much easier to look at Figure 4.1 than the list of ages above. You can easily draw this kind of plot by hand when you first see an array of numbers that is not clear. The x-axis on a histogram is a list of possible outcomes, and the y-axis is the frequency, or count, of each of those observations.

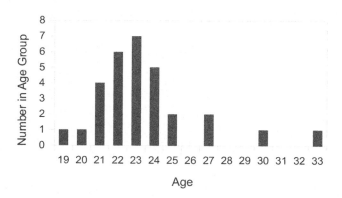

Figure 4.1. Histogram of student ages in a class.

To make understanding these numbers even easier, you can try working with a spreadsheet program like Microsoft Excel or Libre Office Calc. You will be working with spreadsheets whenever you have a large amount of quantitative data because it is easy to deal with the data in this kind of format. Go ahead and type all of the ages listed in the data table into a column in the spreadsheet, starting in the upper left. Select the empty cell after the last observation (cell A30) and type:

=AVERAGE(A1:A29)

then press enter

The program will automatically calculate the average, or mean, for you.

Pick the next empty cell, A31 and type

=MEDIAN(A1:A29)

then press enter

Pick the next empty cell and type

=MODE(A1:A29)

then press enter

As you can see, all of the descriptive values were calculated for you. Try this on your own with a new set of numbers and you can see how easy it is.

Now, with these numbers you have found that the mean is 23.31, the median is 23 and the mode is 23. When the mean, median, and mode are all similar, we can often make another assumption, which is that the data come from a normal distribution. A normal distribution has the same mean, median, and mode. It is symmetrical. Consider the blue line in the graph below.

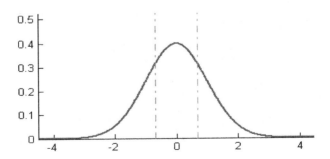

The normal distribution has gone by other names, such as a bell curve or a Gaussian distribution, named after Carl Fredrich Gauss who discovered the mathematics behind the normal distribution. The formula and calculations behind it were derived from calculus and at the time of the discovery, long before computers, it allowed scholars to predict a lot of the behavior of the world. The following are just a few of the things in the world that are normally distributions:

Heights

Weights

Yearly average temperatures

Stock market fluctuations

IQ scores*

Reaction times

In fact, most observations of the natural world are normally distributed. Heights of trees, and brightness of stars in the sky are two examples. But not all things are normally distributed. For instance, look at this small sample of housing prices, and calculate the mean and median.

1,900,000	310,000
390,000	290,000
250,000	240,000
300,000	350,000
2,800,000	310,000

The mean is 714,000, nearly twice as high as the median, which is 310,000! (The mode is also 310,000, but the mode does not always have as much information as the mean and median.) When we have these vastly different numbers, it is useful to ask The cause of this discrepancy is that the observations are biased by the very expensive houses. Even though most homes in this sample cost around 300,000 the two that cost over a million are raising the mean. So the difference between the distribution of ages and the distribution of housing prices is an example of how the mean and median can give us a lot of information.

Now, look at the following set of numbers:

1
2
3
4
5

What is the mode? The mode would be 1, 2, 3, 4 and 5. The mean is 3 and the median is 3, which makes us think that the distribution might be normal. However, having many modes will quash that idea. Three simple calculations, the mean, median, and mode, have been able to give you a lot of information about the numbers they describe. In fact, this last set of numbers looks like a *uniform distribution*. This means that the probability of getting any of the possible outcomes is the same. (Probability is simply the chance of something happening.) Take this set of numbers:

1 2 3 4 5 6

This is the distribution that comes from rolling a fair six-sided die. A fair die will always give you a uniform distribution. What are the chances of getting a "1"? 1/6. There are 6 possible outcomes, and the chances of getting any number on a six-sided die are one in six. This kind of distribution is also called a *discreet distribution* because the distribution is cut into chunks. You can have a "one" or "two" as an outcome, but you can not have one-and-a-half as an outcome. A *continuous distribution* would allow for all possible outcomes. These possible outcomes are either bounded or unbounded. For instance, think of a gas contained within a glass sphere. Now think of one particular molecule of that gas. That molecule of gas can be anywhere inside that sphere, and the probability of it being at each possible location is the same. You can consider each possible location as a point on a continuous line of possible locations for that molecule. This is a *bounded distribution*, as the boundary for the set of possible locations that the molecule can be located is the glass sphere which contains the gas.

Time to work: draw the probability distributions for the following set of situations. You will first need to think about the possible outcomes, and then the likelihood of those possible outcomes.

What do the distributions look like for:

A coin flip

A number on a roulette wheel

Incomes

So, how many possible outcomes are there in a coin flip? Since there are only two possible outcomes and each outcome is equally likely, the possibility space for a coin flip looks like this:

	Heads	Tails
Observations	A	B

Here, A is the number of heads observed, and B is the number of tails observed. To find out the proportion of heads, all you would have to do would be to divide the number of heads by the number of heads plus the number of tails. For a fair coin, A and B would both be ½, or 50%.

4.2 Standard Deviation and Variance

Standard deviation, or SD, and Variance, or Var, are the next descriptives to be defined. These values are going to yield a lot more information about the distributions being analyzed. These numbers are not overwhelming, and these values will be used in more calculations later. Variance is the average of squared differences from the mean. Take the following set of numbers:

2   3   4   5   6

To calculate the variance, first calculate the mean:

mean=$\Sigma x_i/n$, where Σ means sum, x_i means for each value of x, and n means the total number of observations.

mean=(2+3+4+5+6)/5=4

Once the mean is calculated, the next step is to calculate the variance.

Var=$\Sigma(x_i-\mu)/n$ where x_i is each value of x, and μ is the mean.

$(2-4)^2 = 4$

$+(3-4)^2 = 1$

$+(4-4)^2 = 0$

$+(5-4)^2 = 1$

$+(6-4)^2 = 4$

var=10/5=2

var=2

To calculate the standard deviation, take the square root of the variance.

SD=√var

SD=√2

SD=1.4

Standard deviation is a very useful statistic used for calculating the characteristics of the general population. If you have a normal distribution, knowing the mean and standard deviation will let you know what the spread of the distribution looks like. For instance, IQ scores are standardized with a mean of 100 and a standard deviation of 15. The asterisk in the list of examples of a normal distribution above is due to the fact that IQ is not a naturally occurring phenomenon. It is not an objective measure, but a measure based on a man-made test. The scoring methodology is adjusted and monitored so that the average IQ remains 100, and the standard deviation remains 15. Once you know the mean and SD, all sorts of information is available to you now if you are willing to do some simple calculations. For instance, if you want to calculate the range of IQ for half of the population, you start by multiplying the SD by .6745. The value .6745 is a standard value for calculating the middle 50% of the population. Here is where the number .6745 comes from on a normal distribution:

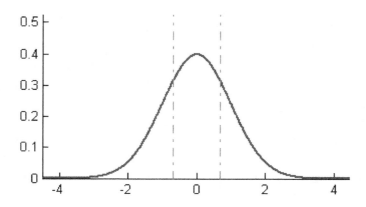

The area under the curve from -.6745 to +.6745 represents .5 of the total area under the whole curve. As you see, in a normal distribution, half of the population is less than one standard deviation from 0.

To find out the range of IQs for the middle 50% of the population, multiply the standard deviation by .6745.

15*.6745=10.12

The number 10.12 is then added and subtracted to the mean.

100+10.12=110.12

100-10.12=89.88

This tells us that half of the population has an IQ between about 89.88 and 110.12. One standard deviation from the mean is written as:

mean ± (1*SD)

What percentage of the population has an IQ within one SD of the mean? Since SD is a standardized measurement, you do not necessarily have to do any complicated calculations. You can look up the information.

Percentage of population within:

.5 SD of the mean: 38.2
1 SD of the mean: 68.2
1.5 SD of the mean: 86.6
2 SD of the mean: 95.4
2.5 SD of the mean: 98.8
3 SD of the mean: 99.8

Now, if you are told that the average height for American women is 5'4" tall and the standard deviation is 3", then you immediately know that 68.2% of the population is between 5'1" and 5'7" tall [5'4"± (1*3")] , and you also know that 95.4% of the population of women is between 4'10" and 5'10" [5'4"± (2*3")]. Almost the entire population of women can be accounted for by 3 SDs, between 4'7" and 6'1", but a small percentage will fall outside of this range.

The calculations for Var and SD can be done very simply in a spreadsheet. Type in the numbers you want to use in the first column in a new sheet. In the next cell, A6 type

=VAR(A1:A5)

then press enter

In the next cell, type

=STDEV(A1:A5)

then press enter

Go back to the values from the ages of students in the class. Try this calculation. The variance of the students ages is 7.96, and the standard deviation is 2.82. Before going on, make sure you can successfully perform this calculation.

The following exercise is an opportunity to test your understanding of some of these concepts, and will introduce some new ones.

Lets start by describing the outcomes of rolling dice. If you know the probabilities of dice, you will be better at most games. So take two dice and roll them. What possible outcomes can you get? For instance, the lowest number you can get is a 2. You can get this value by rolling a 1 on one die and and 1 on the other, so there is only one way to get a 2 with two dice. How about a 3? You can get a 1 on the first die and a 2 on the second, or a 2 on the first die and a 1 on the second.

Create a grid like this, with the top row being the possible outcomes of a roll of the first die, and the column on the left being the possible outcomes of a roll of the second die:

Die 1

	1	2	3	4	5	6
1						
2						
3						
4						
5						
6						

Die 2

Now fill in the grid with all possible combinations.

Die 1

	1	2	3	4	5	6
1	2	3	4	5	6	7
2	3	4	5	6	7	8
3	4	5	6	7	8	9
4	5	6	7	8	9	10
5	6	7	8	9	10	11
6	7	8	9	10	11	12

Die 2

What is the mean, median, and mode of this distribution?

What number or numbers represent the least common possible

outcome?

What does this distribution look like?

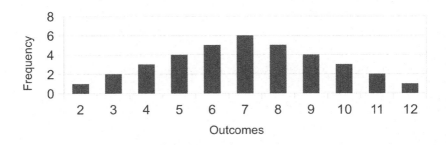

Figure 4.2. Outcome of 2 dice being tossed

This is not a normal distribution, although it might look like one at first glance. This is a special case where two random samples of two uniform distributions form a triangular shape as in Figure 4.2. This is considered an example of the binomial distribution, where the each outcome is generated by two separate (but in this case identical) events.

In order to calculate any individual outcome, you multiply the probability of the outcome on the first die (1/6) by the probability of that outcome on the second die (1/6). Probability is a measure of the likelihood of an occurrence or outcome. Probabilities can be written as fractions.

$1/6 * 1/6 = 1/36$

$.167 * .167 = .0278$

Probabilities can also be written as percentages by multiplying the decimal representation of the fraction by 100.

$.0278 * 100 = 2.78\%$

This is the probability of any one specific outcome of a single throw of two dice. Look at the least likely outcomes, 2 and 12. Each of these can only be generated one way. A two can only be generated by rolling one and one, and at 12 can only be generated by rolling six and six. The probability of getting 2 when rolling two die is therefore 1/36. The probability of getting 12 is also 1/36. The probability of getting other numbers varies in the number of ways it can be generated. Seven, the most common outcome, can be generated six different ways. The probability of getting a seven is therefore 6/36 (1/6), or .167. What is the probability of rolling two sevens in a row?

$1/6 * 1/6 = 1/36$

So even though this is the most common outcome, rolling two sevens in a row has the same likelihood as rolling a 2, or .0278. Gamblers beware, the house always wins.

4.3 Types of Variables

The last topic here is about types of variables. Knowing the types of variables you are dealing with will be very important when you begin doing statistical tests. There are 4 main types of variables: nominal, ordinal, interval, and ratio. These are often referred to as "levels of measurement" or "scales of measurement."

Nominal variables are variables that denote a difference between groups, but that there is no hierarchical difference between them. Race is a good example of a nominal variable. You can put people into different racial categories, but these categories are simply descriptive. They are only described by name, and have no mathematical relationship with other variables.

Ordinal variables allow you to rank them. For instance, finishing order in a marathon is an ordinal variable because there is an order in which people finished the race. Order is the only difference between first, second, and third place.

Interval variables have a consistent difference between the answers. For instance, it is the same distance between 2 and 3 PM as it is between 3 and 4 PM. This is not true for finishers in a marathon, where they are ranked. Second place may be 3 seconds ahead of third place, but third place may be 10 seconds ahead of fourth place! In an interval scale, the distance between each category is equal.

Ratio variables are similar to interval variables, but they have a "true zero." The true zero is the only piece that makes ratio variables different from interval variables. Height and weight are good examples. While no one can actually be zero feet tall or weigh zero pounds, these measures are still in relation to zero. For the purposes of most statistics, interval and ratio variables will be dealt with the same way, so the term *interval-ratio* will often be used to describe both of these variables.

Key Terms

Bounded distribution

Binomial distribution

Data Set

Descriptive statistics

Distribution

Interval variable

Interval-ratio variable

Mean

Median

Mode

Normal distribution

Nominal variable

Ordinal variable

Probability

Ratio variable

Standard deviation

Unbounded distribution

Uniform distribution

Variance

Problems

1) You collect the amount of time, in minutes, it takes people to complete a test. The times are: 23.1, 27.5, 20.1, 24.6, 30.2, 30.1, 26.0, 27.9, 37.2, 22.0, 28.7, 20.6, 25.5, 21.4, and 33.3. Calculate:

a) the mean

b) the median

c) the standard deviation

d) the standard error

Chapter 5

The Experiment: An introduction to the Independent Variable

Topics:

5.1 Introduction and History

5.2 Single Experimental Manipulation with Two Groups

5.3 Sources of Variability: ANOVA Example

5.1 Introduction and History

Conducting an experiment is a fairly new idea in the evolution of research methods. It was not until the mid eighteenth century that Dr. James Lind performed the first human trial experiment with an *independent variable* manipulation. This was the famous study of scurvy in the British Navy. Until that time no one knew the cause of scurvy, a disease which often affected sailors who were at sea for a long time. Symptoms start with fatigue and aching, and end up leading to tremors, blackened skin, and gangrenous flesh, and death. Hippocrates, the Greek father of medicine, had written that illness was caused by an imbalance of the four humors: blood, phlegm, yellow bile, and black bile. This led others to suggest that scurvy was a disease of the spleen, which was blocked and led to an increase in black bile. While this may seem nonsensical to us today, just three hundred years ago this was good medical science.

Sailor's rations consisted mostly of bread, meat, and beer, which led Lind to suggest a dietary change. He tested six different possible treatments on twelve patients. He gave groups of two patients that had scurvy symptoms one of the following treatments: cider, vitriol, vinegar, sea water, nutmeg, or citrus fruits. Of course, the patients that received citrus fruits were so much better in just a few days that they were able to start taking care of the other patients. Still, Lind's findings were not immediately published or accepted. Today, we know that scurvy is caused by a diet low in vitamin C, and that citrus fruits are high in vitamin C. Modern drug trials are run in a similar way, with treatments randomized among patients. In Lind's study, the independent variable was the treatment, and the *dependent variable* was the health of the patient.

James Lind's Scurvy Study

Hypothesis: Scurvy is caused by a diet deficient in citrus fruits.

IV: Diet, 6 levels: cider, vitriol, vinegar, sea water, nutmeg, citrus fruits

DV: Health, severity of symptoms

Survey data, preexisting data, and observational data are all inferior to the experimental data in one key way: analysis of experimental data can be used to show causation. It is much more difficult to demonstrate causation in other types of research. Even when you create a good survey and try to control for other variables, other possible explanations, there might still be another variable that is responsible for the effect you observed. This is called the "third-variable problem" and refers to the fact that you think that two variables are related, but in fact both are actually related to a third. Since there are a number of other variables that may have an effect on your IV or DV, these variables are often called "control variables" and are measured as part of the design of the study in order to see just how much of an effect they really have.

For example, a researcher thinks that drowning is related to eating. She collects a great deal of data and finds that there are more reported drownings when ice-cream sales go up. The researcher thinks that this is good evidence that she is correct. When more ice-cream is sold, more people drown. She writes up her results in a paper and said that your mom was right; you should wait at least half an hour after eating before going swimming.

What? Let's ignore the obvious problem with the researcher's logical reasoning, and try to solve the problem of relating ice-cream sales to the increase in drowning. In fact, there is a third-variable responsible for the researcher's data linking ice-cream sales to drowning. In the summer, people generally eat more ice-cream and swim more. This does not mean that one causes the other. Stating that one thing causes our observed finding when in fact the results are caused by something else is called an *attribution error*. In Figure 5.1, the dotted line represents the attribution error.

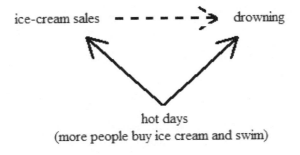

Figure 5.1. Example of the 3rd Variable Problem

Demonstrating causation in an experiment, however, is rather easy by comparison. In fact, the reason that you perform an experiment is so that you can test whatever explanation you think is responsible for the observations. You create an experimental group and a control group and randomly assign those who are participating in your experiment to one of the groups. Another option is to assign people to more than one condition.

5.2 Single Experimental Manipulation with Two Groups

This example will walk you through the design of a study and the analysis associated. We address the statistics and SPSS analysis here so that by the end of this section you will have all of the tools necessary to design and analyze your own two-group study. For this example, you will be interested in determining how a subject will vote based on their knowledge of a candidate. You think that people will be less likely to vote for a candidate that had a recent affair. You carefully control the conditions, and you create two readings. One reading is a list of the accomplishments of the candidate and includes some personal information like the candidate's schooling and his family. The other list has exactly the same information as the first, but includes a sentence stating that the candidate had an affair with a staff member last year and has apologized to his family and constituents. This way, the only difference between the two lists has to do with the manipulation of the IV. You ask twenty-one people to rate how likely they would be to vote for the candidate on the following scale:

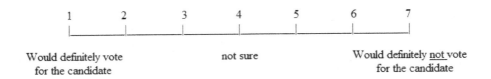

Would definitely vote for the candidate   not sure   Would definitely <u>not</u> vote for the candidate

Half of the people get the first story, and half of the people get the second story. You get the following data:

No affair   2,3,2,1,2,1,1,4,4,3

Affair   4,5,7,6,6,5,4,4,3,4,5

Each number in the 'Affair' and 'No Affair' groups corresponds to a different person who was given the reading and asked to make a judgement. You do not need equal size groups for this kind of test, but the groups should be fairly equivalent in size. It is not unusual to have a few more subjects in one group. For the analysis, you must be clear on the type of data you have. For the *independent samples t-test*, you must have data that form a normal distribution and are either interval or ratio that come from a normal distribution. (Note: We will use a t-test to analyze this data, but it may not always be the best test. For example, with ratings collected from the political readings, it might be best to use a *Mann-Whitney test*. Like the independent t-test, it can be used on between-subjects data. Unlike the independent t-test, however, the results of a rating experiment may not be normally distributed data and are not interval or ratio data. The characteristics of the data do not fit the required parameters to use a t-test. These tests will be discussed more fully in Chapter 8.)

We are going to use the IBM SPSS Statistics Package for all of our complex statistical calculations. When using the IBM SPSS, remember that you must enter your variables in a certain way: columns represent variables, while rows represent subjects. Each row is a separate subject, and each column represents a particular measure of that subjects. Remember this to make sure you have entered data correctly.

You must also perform a bit of recoding. Each score must have an additional number associated with it. This new number represents the group to which the subject was assigned. For instance, the first three values from the no affair story would look like this:

1	2
1	3
1	2

The first three values from the affair story would look like this:

2	4
2	5
2	7

For the independent-samples t-test, it does not matter what number you put in the first column, as long as it is the same for all members of each condition. It is a grouping variable. The only meaning it holds is to assign the observed score to a group. In other words, it is a nominal variable. In this case, we use "1" for group 1 and "2" for group 2. We could just have easily used "100" for group one and "57" for group two. The number is arbitrary.

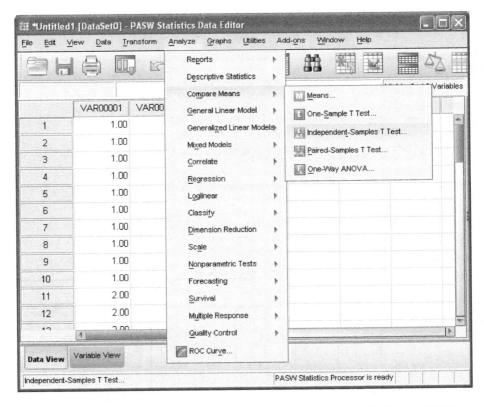

(*Reprint courtesy of International Business Machines Corporation, © SPSS, Inc., an IBM Company.)

Now click on analyze, compare means, and independent-samples t test.

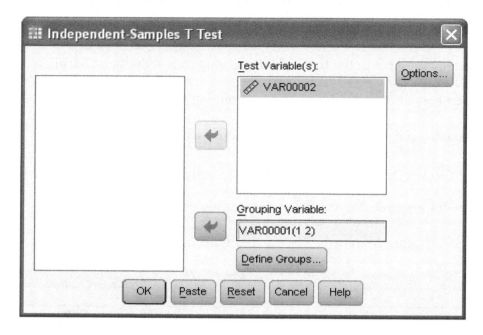

Remember that variable 1 is your grouping variable. Define groups by the arbitrary numbers you used in variable 1: "no affair" was coded as a 1, and "affair" was coded as a 2. You just have to tell the program that you want to compare groups 1 and 2.

Your SPSS output is below.

Independent Samples Test

	Levene's Test for Equality of Variances		t-test for Equality of Means						
								95% Confidence Interval of the Difference	
	F	Sig.	t	df	Sig. (2-tailed)	Mean Difference	Std. Error Difference	Lower	Upper
Equal variances assumed	.017	.899	-4.952	19	.000	-2.51818	.50852	-3.58253	-1.45383
Equal variances not assumed			-4.954	18.836	.000	-2.51818	.50834	-3.58278	-1.45358

For now we will ignore Levene's Test for Equality of Variances. Just keep it in mind for later. For now, look at the "Equality of variances assumed" box. The three numbers we care about here are circled: the t, df, and sig. (p-value).

A couple quick notes: IBM SPSS always reports the 2-tailed p-value here. Let's go back to our hypothesis: people will be less likely to vote for a candidate that had a recent affair. This is a 1-tailed test, so divide a 2-tailed p-value by 2. Here, it is reported as .000, but it is not actually zero. It is just very small. A p-value will never, ever be zero. *Always report a p-value that is very tiny as <.001, never as p = .000.*

Report your results as $t(19) = -4.952$, $p<.001$. Time for one more step: we believe the "affair" group should have a higher score, meaning they would be less likely to vote for the candidate. You have to look at the means yourself, and make sure that subjects did score higher in that condition. Otherwise, you could think you're right, when you're actually completely wrong! It may seem unlikely to think people would be more likely to vote for a candidate who had an affair, but often in research we discover things we believed to be true are, in fact, false. If you lived a thousand years ago, you would believe the world is flat!

Notice that the t is negative. This is merely a measure of directionality. It tells you only that the first group has a smaller mean than the second group. If the t-score was positive, it would mean that the first group had a larger mean rank than the second group. This makes sense with the data here, since you expect that the no affair group would give as their rating a smaller number, which would make their average smaller than the affair group. The important information about the size of the t-score is the absolute value of the t-score. Here, it is 4.952, which is very large.

How large is 4.952? The plot below shows the probability density of a t that large on a t-distribution with 19 degrees of freedom. The vertical dashed line shows where the t-score would appear on the plot. Note that most of the area under the curve is between -2 and 2 (negative 2 and positive 2). If there was no difference between the groups, the dashed line would be near zero.

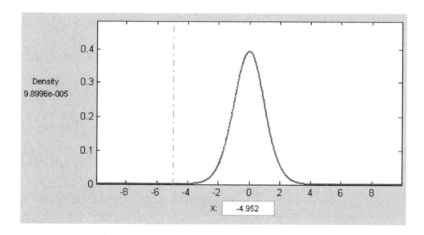

To do the Mann-Whitney test in SPSS, the data can be organized the same way as for the independent samples t-test. Go to Analyze/Non-parametric tests/2-independent samples.

When doing the Mann-Whitney test for independent samples, the score you report would be the z-score and the p-value, as well as the reported ranks.

$$z = -3.439, p<.001$$

The mean rank for the no affair group was 6.20, and the mean rank for the affair group was 15.36.

The z-score here is negative. Like a negative t-value, this only denotes directionality, based on the order you put the variables into SPSS. A z-score is a standardization of data used to make comparisons. It denotes the number of standard deviations away from the mean something is. Here, your data is over three standard deviations from the mean. Any data point can be given a z-score by simply subtracting the mean from the data point and dividing the answer by the standard deviation.

Note that in this study, once the subject saw one scenario, they could not be presented with the second scenario or it would be clear what the researcher was looking for and the results might be influenced by the demand characteristic. Sometimes, that need not be the case. The next example will deal subjects being presented with more than one experimental manipulation.

5.3 Sources of Variability, ANOVA Example

As noted, once you achieve a change in your subject's behavior, you can no longer give your subject the other condition, since a change has already occurred and might be irreversible. However, sometimes this is not the case.

The difference between these two basic experimental models is that one is called a *within-subjects* experiment and one is called a *between-subjects* experiment. For a within-subjects experiment, each subject is given all conditions, also called treatments, of an experiment. The variability in behavior is due to the variability *within* each individual's behavior (you don't always behave the same way in the same situation. For between-subjects, each subject is given only one condition. The variability in behavior is due to differences *between* individuals (you and your friend score differently on tests).

One of the advantages of a within subjects experiment is that each subject serves as his or her own control. A good example of a within-subjects experiment is a memory experiment. Memory is the variable of interest, with some people having a much better memory for word lists than other people. In order to avoid the problem of individual differences, each subject is tested on all conditions. The assumption we must make is that one condition will not have any effect on the next condition, but in order to control for this the word lists are randomly assigned. It is important to assume that one condition not be expected to have a big effect on the other conditions. Each subject sees the same things but in a different order. In this case, a linguist wants to know if the memory for words is influenced by how the words are related. The researcher is studying phonological relations between words, and creates lists that are related on rhyme and overlap in the syllable, as well as creating a control condition where none of the words are related. The researcher wants to test whether people have better memory for words that end with the same sound compared to words that begin with the same sound and words that neither begin or end with the same sound. Examples of lists are given below:

Rhyme   yam lamb ham dam cam ram jam

Overlap   bag bat back bash bad bath bass

Unrelated   moon gill tack cone gate wood year

After controlling for word frequency (how often a word is used per million occurrences in the language), density (how many words are phonologically related to a word), and probability (the likelihood of one phonological sound following another), the researcher creates many lists and tests his subjects on all of them and collects the number of words remembered for each list. Then the researcher adds the number remembered for each category together, as presented in Table 5.1:

Table 5.1: Total number of words that each subject remembered for each type of list

subject	rhyme	overlap	unrelated
1	15	11	10
2	17	10	9
3	19	14	15
4	14	11	10
5	16	11	11

This type of data can be analyzed using an analysis of variance, usually referred to as an ANOVA. The particular type of ANOVA is a repeated-measures ANOVA, which takes into account the fact that each subject is acting as his or her own control. The data in Table 1 could be input into SPSS and analyzed with a one-way ANOVA. Performing this test yields the following statistic:

$F(2,8) = 44.07$, p<.001.

This F-statistic and associated p-value tells us that there is a difference between the groups. It does not, however, tell us what the differences are, or which differences are significant. To determine the nature of the differences, the researcher must perform tests between each of the three conditions. While contrast tests can be performed in many ways, in order to limit the number of processes described here the dependent-t-test will be used. Each subject performs each condition, making this a within subjects test. The formula for this test

is very simple:

$$t(df) = \Sigma D / \sqrt{[(n\Sigma D^2-(\Sigma D)^2)/n-1]}$$

where ΣD is the sum of the differences between each set of numbers

and df is the *degrees of freedom*. There are theoretical implications for

the degrees of freedom, but for the purposes here they are used as a

number that allows the t value that they are associated with to be

looked up in a table in order to find the appropriate p-value. The df is

calculated in a *paired-samples t-test* by subtracting 1 from the total

number of subjects. That leaves 4 in this case.

subject	rhyme	overlap	D	D^2
1	15	11	4	16
2	17	10	7	49
3	19	14	5	25
4	14	11	3	9
5	16	11	5	25
			$\Sigma D= 24$	$\Sigma D^2= 124$

$t(4) = 24 / \sqrt{[(5*124-576)/4]}$

$t(4) = 24/3.3167$

$t(4) = 7.236$

In order to find whether this is a significant difference, look up the critical value of t with 4 degrees of freedom at the .05 level. When looking up the critical value, you are required to use a one-tailed test or a two-tailed test. This difference will not be addressed here, but we will use a two-tailed test here.

rhyme-overlap t(4)=7.236, p=.002

and for the other two:

rhyme-unrelated t(4)=7.076, p=.002

overlap-unrelated t(4)=1.000, p=.374

Now we can see that the number of words remembered from the rhyme list is greater than the number of words remembered from both the overlap and unrelated lists, but that the number of words remembered from the overlap list is not significantly different from the number of words remembered from the unrelated list.

This type of t-test is deceptive in its complexity, since performing the algebra in order to get the t-value is a simple task.

A between-subjects experiment is different mathematically, because each subject does not act as her own control. The study with the political candidates is an example of a between-subjects experiment. Another good example of the use of the between-subjects experimental model is pharmaceutical drug testing. Since exposure to one pharmaceutical compound may cause an irreversible change in the participant, a separate group is required for each condition. The mathematics is different as well, and will not be covered here. In addition, when doing contrast analysis a researcher must be aware of the type of experiment that they are doing. A dependent t-test analysis on between-subjects data will yield incorrect results, while an independent t-test analysis on within-subjects examples will also yield incorrect results. You have all of the tools now to reproduce the politician study on your own, as well as the ability to analyze and interpret the results.

The experiment is used more often in some fields in social science than others. For instance, Experimental Psychology heavily relies on this methodology in order to draw conclusions about the human cognition. The example of the memory study that relied on word lists given earlier is an example of a classical experimental psychology design. The results of a study like this could increase our understanding of how human memory works. In Social Psychology and Sociology, the experiment can be used to understand human behavior or to understand the behavior of groups. A study need not be complicated. The example of the politician study where the only difference in two scenarios was that in one scenario the politician having had an affair could and in understanding how people really feel about a real life situation.

To summarize, the key to the experiment is the manipulation of the independent variable. You assign your subjects to groups and decide which group gets which level of the independent variable, or you give each subject all conditions and measure the different response to each condition. As the researcher, you are able to control which subject gets which variable when, and you are then able to demonstrate causation by tying the effect to the independent variable and nothing else.

Key Terms

attribution error

between-subjects

confound

degrees of freedom

dependent variable

grouping variable

independent variable

Mann-Whitney test

Independent samples t-test

Paired samples t-test

third-variable problem

within-subjects

Exercises

For each of the following, construct scenarios and hold all other variables constant.

1. Design a study where you describe a crime and you change the sex of the perpetrator to determine if people rate the perpetrator as more or less guilty depending on their sex, or try changing the sex of the victim and determine if this effects the way people perceive the crime.

2. Design a study where you determine if people think a minor should be punished less than a person over 18 for committing the same crime. Design a study to see if people think a senior citizen should be punished less than a 25-year old for committing the same crime.

3. Design a study where you determine if people are more likely to agree with a famous person.

4. Design a study where you determine if people are more likely to vote for a male or a female political candidate.

Chapter 6

The Survey: Collecting Information about People

Topics:

6.1 Introduction to the Survey

The survey is an old data collection technique. It is hard to say when the first survey was given, but those familiar with the Judaic, Christian, or Islamic traditions knows that over 2000 years ago Mary and Joseph had to travel to Bethlehem because the Roman government was conducting a census. There was no room at any of the inns because people all over the region were required to go to the towns of their heritage in order to be counted for the purpose of taxation and military service. Historically, this was the census of Quirinis, who was then the regional governor appointed during the reign of Caesar

Augustus. This was not the first recorded census: the Roman government had been conducting censuses since 500 years BC. The census is a survey used to count the number of people living in a region, but it can also be used to count the number of animals or take a count of any other information, such as ownership of land or food reserves.

The United States census has been conducted since the Presidency of George Washington. The constitution requires that the census be taken, and the results of the census dictate how many representatives each state sends to the US House of Representatives.

Title 13 of the US Code requires a head count, though it has been argued that statistical sampling techniques are both cheaper and more accurate. The constitution is not clear on the actual method for conducting the census, so the argument between those supporting using a head count and those supporting statistical sampling are political arguments. The Government Accountability Office estimates that the cost of the 2010 US Census as 13.7-14.5 billion dollars (GAO, 2010). Obviously, the US census is an extremely important tool, as the number of representatives from each state and the amount of federal money sent to the states relies on it. For the purpose of scientific research, the best sampling methods should be employed. Political concerns should be irrelevant in conducting the census or any survey. (The two questions influenced by politics are: Who is being undersampled? Who would want those groups to continue to be undersampled?)

It seems to the average person that counting every American should be the best way to take a census. Contrary to logic, however, counting heads is not as good a measure as statistical sampling with as sample as large as the United States population. This is partly due to the fact that with over 300 million people to count, it is difficult to count every single one. Many people are missed every year by the census. Some people do not want to be counted (i.e., fugitives), and some people are difficult to find (i.e., the homeless). A head count can not spend enough to make sure that every person on the margins is counted. A good statistical sample, however, requires that each person selected *must* be counted and more money can be spent in order to make sure each person is counted. When the numbers are generalized to the population, there is an extremely small *sampling error*. The sampling error is the difference between the statistical mean calculated by the sample and the actual population mean.

The sampling error is a measure of how close your sample is to the actual population. Take a political poll, for instance. Generally the numbers are reported as follows:

Candidate A   54%

Candidate B   49%

Sampling error +/- 4 percentage points

Does this mean that candidate A is assured a win? The numbers are higher. The sampling error, however, creates a kind of interval. It means that Candidate A's real score is between 50 and 58, and that Candidate B's real score is between 45 and 53. Since these ranges overlap, you can not be sure that Candidate A will win, or has the most support. It is possible that the real score for Candidate A is as low as 50, and that the real score for Candidate B is as high as 53! Usually, the larger your sample, the smaller the sampling error you find. This means that generally, the more people you sample, the closer your sample mean is to the true population mean.

Voting is a type of survey, as it is a count of people who support a candidate or proposal. The survey is one of the most common tools used for data collection in the Social Sciences. It is usually the tool of choice when conducting Sociological research, as it is easy to customize for collecting specific information about groups and social issues. Usually the information being collected is used to make a statement about the relationship between groups. If done correctly, a survey can be highly informative. For example, businesses have been collecting information about what people like in order to guide their development of products since before WWII, and political campaigns have been conducting polls in order to help shape their message and make their candidate electable. Companies want to know what people want to buy so they can sell that product, and candidates want to know what issues are important to people so they can get people's attention.

Surveys are excellent tools in the social sciences because they are relatively inexpensive and useful for describing the characteristics of a large population. Often, the researcher does not have to be present, and a well-designed survey can avoid subjectivity in answers. A survey must be carefully constructed in order to make sure questions are clear.

The ability to develop and conduct a survey for research purposes is therefore a highly marketable skill; note the examples above in politics, marketing, and social research. Creating a good survey, however, requires a great deal of work. While a survey can seem like just someone asking questions, the preparation involved before a survey can be deployed is quite specific. Some techniques are better than others. Consider sampling techniques, and to the population you ask to take your survey. For instance, the Literary Digest had a history of predicting the winner in presidential elections, when in 1936 it predicted that Alfred Landon would defeat Franklin Delano Roosevelt in the presidential election. The mistaken prediction was due to the way the poll was conducted. The magazine sent out 10 million surveys to its readers, and 2.4 million people responded. Of those that responded, clearly most of them preferred Alfred Landon for president. Can you see why this sample may not be fully representative of the U.S. Population? Sampling techniques will be explained more thoroughly in Section 6.6.

6.2 Survey Design and Asking Questions

Before a survey can be conducted, it must be carefully designed to insure that we get the best information possible from the survey. Of course, in order to design a good survey, one must start with a good research question. This has been addressed in the chapter on the hypothesis. Assuming that the hypothesis has been well developed, it is now time to go through the development of the survey.

For example, you want to collect a lot of information about a person: in particular you want to collect information about how many classes a person has taken in college. You could ask a question like one of the following questions:

(1) How many courses have you taken in college? ____

(2) How many courses have you taken in college?

≤5	6-10	11-15	16-20	21-25	26-30	31-35	36-40	40<

Example (1) requires a person to write in the number of classes they have taken. This is referred to as an *open-ended question*.

Example (2) requires a person to merely circle the appropriate response. This is called a *closed-ended question*. There are good reasons to use both types of questions in a survey. For instance, the data collected from an open-ended question will tend to be more precise and allow for a more powerful statistical test. However, use of a closed-ended question might be easier for people to fill out, since they can estimate the number of classes they have taken, or count the number of semesters they have been in college. Closed-ended questions must offer respondents an option for all possible answers, and not overlap. In addition, closed-ended questions allow you to standardize responses. An open-ended question is particularly useful when you want to collect data on opinions and you are not sure how people will react. The following two questions are different kinds of questions that we might include in a survey.

(3) Do you support universal healthcare?
a) No, it is too expensive.
b) No, people should be able to choose whether or not they want healthcare.
c) Yes, the financial burden of illness is too great to not have healthcare.
d) Yes, healthcare is a human right and all people should have access to it.

(4) Do you support universal healthcare?   Yes   No
Why or why not?

In sample question (3), a closed-ended question, the person is required to choose from one of the preselected categories. While adding more categories might be helpful, it may be impossible to think of all alternative responses a person might give. The open-ended question in sample question (4) is much harder to analyze because each person's response must be considered separately. However, if you are collecting a small sample of data and want to really know what people's opinions are, then it might be the best choice. The answers to a survey question should be *exhaustive*, meaning that any possible answer can be given. In yes/no questions, two choices are all the possibilities that need to be given. Answers should also be *mutually exclusive*, meaning that people should not be able to honestly choose more than one answer. To avoid biases', questions should also be balanced, offering positive and negative choices equally.

Another type of question requires people to answer only if they answered a previous question in a certain way. This is referred to as a *filter question* and an example is below in (5).

(5) Do you support universal healthcare?   Yes   No
If yes, please explain why:

Note that these questions have all been clear and straightforward. Care must be taken to avoid asking questions that are heavy in jargon or technical language that lay people might not understand. Another thing to avoid is making multiple statements in one question and then asking for a specific response because it may be unclear to the respondent exactly what they are responding to. An example of this type of question, referred to as a *double-barreled question* is given in (6).

(6) If Iran continues to build its nuclear program and continues to fail to protect human rights, the United States might be forced to go to war with Iran, which would be wrong.
Agree   Disagree

As is demonstrated in this example, the question is not necessarily unclear, but what is unclear is what the respondent is expected to answer because a single question has multiple parts. Do they agree that the U.S. might be forced to go to war with Iran, or that it would be wrong to do so?

Leading questions might make people respond in a certain way. Questions (7) and (8) both have bias, but one is more subtle.

(7) Don't you agree that the police should be able to do anything necessary to protect good, including entering homes without a warrant?   Yes   No

(8) Do you agree that the police should be able to enter homes without a warrant since only criminals would oppose such a law?
Yes   No

Sample question (7) suggests that one answer is preferable, but sample question (8) suggests that anyone who disagrees with the statement is a criminal! Sample question 8 is also an example of a *false premise,* since it is not true that the law against illegal searches and seizures is only supported by criminals; it is also protection against a totalitarian government. (The word *premise* refers to the basis for an argument. In the case above, the basis was *false.*)

If you bias your questions, your respondents may not respond honestly, and they may become angry that you are making untrue assumptions. Another problem that you might encounter is that people might not want to answer a question because the question is too personal. Asking people about their histories with sex, drug use, or arrests may not yield honest answers because people may be embarrassed to respond.

Biased language is another reason for bad data. Think about the statements in the two questions given below, and decide which one you agree with more:

(9) AIDS victims should be eligible for financial help in paying for healthcare.

(10) The government should pay healthcare costs for AIDS patients.

The language in the two questions is dramatically different. In sample question (9), people with AIDS are called victims and the cost associated is referred to as assistance. It is difficult to argue that victims do not deserve help. In sample question (10), they are called patients and it is stated that the government should pay for them. It is more difficult to get support in this case, as people would be less likely to agree that the government should support a particular group of patients. Be cautious in choosing the wording in your questions, as it often influences the responses that you get.

In putting a *questionnaire* together, also be aware that the order of your questions might affect the answers you get. Order effects happen when one question influences the answer to a question that comes later. You can test this out by trying out different question orders and seeing if you get vastly different responses.

6.3 The Index

An index is a way of measuring a concept when there isn't a single question that will measure the concept. It is generally a series of questions that produces a single score for each respondent. This type of data is ordinal, as it allows you to rank your participants upon some dimension. Often, asking your subjects to answer a single question will not get you a specific answer to your question. For example, suppose your research question requires you to find out if people who have better self-esteem also had more parental interaction when they were children. There are two things that must be measured in such a study: the frequency with which their parents interacted with them when they were children, and a measure of self esteem. What question can be asked that will allow you to characterize someone's self esteem? What question will allow you to characterize the amount of interaction that someone's parents had with them?

Now, if you did want to conduct a survey where you measure self-esteem, you do not have to develop a whole new way of asking questions. For example, one way to measure self-esteem is to use Rosenberg's Self-Esteem scale, which can be used freely for educational and research purposes:

		1. STRONGLY AGREE	2. AGREE	3. DIS-AGREE	4. STRONGLY DISAGREE
1.	I feel that I'm a person of worth, at least on an equal plane with others.	SA	A	D	SD
2.	I feel that I have a number of good qual-ities.	SA	A	D	SD
3.	All in all, I am inclined to feel that I am a failure.	SA	A	D	SD
4.	I am able to do things as well as most other people.	SA	A	D	SD
5.	I feel I do not have much to be proud of.	SA	A	D	SD
6.	I take a positive attitude toward myself.	SA	A	D	SD
7.	On the whole, I am satisfied with my-self.	SA	A	D	SD
8.	I wish I could have more respect for myself.	SA	A	D	SD
9.	I certainly feel useless at times.	SA	A	D	SD
10.	At times I think I am no good at all.	SA	A	D	SD

Rosenberg's Self-Esteem Scale

To score Rosenberg's Scale, give the following number of points for the items in 1, 2, 4, 6, and 7: Strongly agree = 3, Agree = 2, Disagree = 1, Strongly disagree = 0. For items 3, 5, 8, 9, and 10 give the following number of points: Strongly agree = 0, Agree = 1, Disagree = 2, Strongly disagree = 3. Items 3, 5, 8, 9, and 10 are *reverse coded*. This means that answering SA to these questions means the same thing as answering SD to the other questions. Reverse coding is a good idea on an index because it avoids having respondents lock into a response. For instance, if they answering "agree" to every question in a set, they might stop reading subsequent questions thoroughly and just answer agree.

There are many such measures that have been developed, so search the literature for what might be available to you in doing your particular research. It is much easier to start with a well established, well developed tool than to develop one yourself.

An index must measure a single construct. Say you want to measure depression. You decide sleep disruption is indicative of depression. However, instead of asking if someone experienced sleep disruption, you ask if someone sleeps more than nine hours a night. While it may be true that some depressed people sleep a lot, it is also true that a lot of non-depressed people sleep nine or more hours a night. This means that your index is also measuring whether or not people sleep a lot, not just depression.

A good way to measure whether your index is being consistent is to use a statistical measure. Cronbach's alpha is a good measure of whether an index is measuring a single construct or multiple constructs. This means it is a measure of *reliability*. Cronbach's alpha is calculated by comparing all "split-half correlations." Take Rosenberg's self esteem scale, for instance. What Cronbach's alpha does is take all combinations of five questions from the survey and compares that with the other five questions from the survey. This means calculating the correlation of questions 1,2,3,4 and 5 with questions 6,7,8,9 and 10, and then calculating the correlation of questions 2,3,4,5 and 6 with questions 7,8,9,10 and 1, through all possible combinations. Fortunately, most statistical programs like SPSS will do this for you with the click of a mouse. Before including your index in your survey, it is useful to do a pilot study by giving your index to people in the population you want to sample and running the Cronbach's alpha test to make sure you are measuring only a single construct. It is almost impossible to create a perfect index in one attempt, so it is important to carefully consider any issues that may arise in using your index. As noted, creating a good, useful, survey does take a lot of work.

Usually, reliability is mentioned with another concept, called *validity*. Validity means you are studying what you think you are studying. A good example of this is when a researcher says they are studying a certain topic, but their operationalizations and measures do not match their conceptualizations. For instance, a research says they are studying compassion, but as a measure of compassion they measure whether or not people eat meat. In this case, it is hard to argue that eating meat means that a person is not compassionate, so there is a disconnect between the concept of compassion and the measure. This disconnect between the conceptualization and the measure leads to a failure of validity. Recall the importance of carefully defining your constructs and linking them to observable operationalizations and the actual measures. Failure to skip this important step can lead to the collection of meaningless data.

6.4 The Scale

There is another tool used in survey measures called the scale. It is more difficult to use than the index for a number of reasons. Generally, it requires you to know a lot more about the topic.

Warning: people often use the terms "index" and "scale" interchangeably. They are NOT the same thing. An example is Rosenberg's self-esteem scale: by our definition, though it is called a scale, it is actually an index!

In an index, you are measuring a single, abstract construct. You assume the each of the questions are related. Consider the self-esteem index: in measuring self esteem, you would assume that a person who feels like they have worth probably also feels like they have a number of good qualities. While this may not be the case for everyone all the time, it is probably true. Both questions are attempting to measure the underlying construct called "self esteem."

In a scale, the rules can change. For instance, a "media consumption scale" can attempt to measure the total amount of media consumed. You may ask how much TV they watch, how much radio they listen to, how much time they spend reading the newspaper, etc. Combining the time a person spends on various forms of media may ba good measure of media consumption, but it may not be true that those who read the newspaper also watch TV. The questions in a such a "media consumption scale" may be a good measure, but may have a low internal consistency score using a test like Cronbach's alpha.

Another type of scale can offer a relationship between the items in the scale, where there is a clear response pattern between the items. In a Guttman scale, agreement with certain items imply agreement with others. Take for example the Bogardus Social Distance scale, an old but widely used scale. The wording below is taken directly from his 1926 paper. People were asked to consider a minority group, and whether they would allow any of the following:

(1) to admit to close kinship by marriage

(2) to have as "chums"

(3) to have as neighbors on the same street

(4) to admit as members of one's occupation within one's country

(5) to admit as citizens of one's country

(6) to admit as visitors only to one's country

(7) to exclude entirely from one's country

In this type of measure, it seems clear that if you would allow someone to be a citizen, you would also allow them to visit your country. If you would not want to have them as a "chum," you would also not want them to marry into your family.

Creating an index or scale requires a great deal of work. Consider the question you want to ask before deciding on the type of measure to use.

6.5 Survey Stats

Statistical information collected from a survey takes two main forms. One is comparing two groups to see if they are different, and the other is looking for a relationship between two variables.

Consider the first case, taking one nominal variable and one interval variable. Rosenberg's Self-Esteem Scale provides data that can be considered interval data, and if you want to look at the difference in Self Esteem scores for men and women, you could do an independent samples ttest. Each individual will give you two pieces of information: sex and a Self Esteem score. (Note: not all researchers agree that index data can be analyzed as interval data, and they may consider it ordinal data. A medians test can be used here, such as the Mann-Whitney.

Often, researchers will perform both an independent samples ttest and a Mann-Whitney U test due to these theoretical objections.)

The second case involves two interval variables. For this example, see if people who are taller have higher Self Esteem. Here you have two interval variables and you want to see the relationship between variables. This requires a test of correlation. For two interval or ratio variables, a Pearson's correlation test can be used. (Note: since it can be argued that index data should be treated as ordinal data, a test that does not require normal, interval-ratio data can be used, such as Kendall's Tao.) These tests are thoroughly explained in the chapter on statistics.

Of course, descriptive statistics are also used. It is useful to report the means and standard deviations of different groups, as well as sample sizes. Often, this information can allow someone experienced in statistics to understand how your groups are similar or different.

6.6 Sampling

In any study, the researcher must have an understanding of where she will get her data. Obviously, only in a few rare cases will every member of the population be counted. The US census, for political reasons, attempts to count every head, when sampling will cost less and be just as accurate or may be even more accurate. The only time a researcher might wish to sample all members of a population is when that population is very small. Otherwise, it may be prohibitively time consuming, difficult, or expensive to sample the entire population. The ideal course of action is to sample some members of a population and use them to represent the whole population.

The two main types of sample that will be discussed are the *random sample* and the n*on-random sample*. When random sampling is possible, it is best to do that. The random sample assumes that every subject has an equal probability of being included in the study group. It requires you to assign a number to every member of a population that you could conceivably sample, and then take a random sample of those members. How would you take a random sample of the entire United States population? How would you take a random sample of the population of your town?

Random samples can be prohibitively expensive and time consuming, so often non-random samples are used. Non-random samples are never as good as random samples, but are often used because they are more convenient. In fact, the first type of non-random sample is called a *convenience sample* and it describes a sample comprised of whomever you could find to sample. It is like sampling your friends, classmates, or just going outside and getting the first fifty people willing to talk to you and fill out a survey. It is easy to do, but least representative of the population.

A *quota sample* is a better sample than a convenience sample. Say you want to see how much students at your college enjoy their classes. First, you would need to create a measure of "enjoyment of classes," probably an index. Then, you might want to identify key demographics of your college so that you can get a decent representation of the population. Perhaps your university has the racial and gender demographics as in Table 1.

Key demographics and survey size

	Male	Female
Asian	15%	15%
Black	5%	5%
Hispanic	15%	15%
White	15%	15%
		Total 100%

If you were going to sample 100 people at your college and wanted to represented the racial and gender makeup of the population, you would then sample 15 male Asians, 15 female Asians, etc. You could fill your quotas in any way you like, perhaps by standing outside a building and surveying the first 15 male Asians to enter, the first 15 female Asians to enter, etc., until you had filled your quotas.

Another type of non-random sample is the *purposive sample*. These are often used to survey special or hard to reach populations. A purposive sample is any method you use to get your respondents, and is often necessary if the group you are looking for is a small, special group. For instance, perhaps you want to measure a small, specific group, such as cabdrivers. If you went out in the population and just started asking people if they drove a cab, this study could take a lifetime. Instead, it would be useful to plan out how you would measure this group, and proceed with a "purpose" by visiting a dispatcher or a place where taxis often pick up passengers.

A special type of purposive sample is the *snowball sample*. An example of a hard to reach population can be a group engaged in illegal activity. For instance, researchers are forced to use special techniques to reach these difficult populations. For instance, Baskin-Sommers & Sommers (2006) used a snowball sample to study methamphetamine users. They paid each interviewee, and the interviewees referred other methamphetamine users that they knew. It might be very difficult to find many methamphetamine users, but methamphetamine users know each other, and that existing network can be used to increase the sample size.

Key Terms

Biased language

Closed-ended question

Convenience sample

Correlation

False premise

Filter question

Double-barreled question

Independent samples ttest

Index

Interval (or ratio) variable

Leading question

Nominal variable

Non-random sample

Open-ended question

Ordinal variable

Purposive sample

Questionnaire

Quota sample

Random sample

Reliability

Reverse coding

Sample

Snowball sample

Validity

Problems

1) You are hired by a politician who wants to find out if he might be a popular candidate.

What kinds of questions would you ask?

Who would you sample?

2) A company wants to find out how to market a new flavor of soda. How could they best conduct this study? Consider:

How would they find out to whom to market the product?

Where would be the best place to sell the product?

For how much could they sell product?

References

Baskin-Sommers, A. & Sommers, I. 2006. Methamphetamine use and violence among young adults. *Journal of Criminal Justice.* 34(6) 661-674

Bogardus, E. S. 1926. Social Distance in the City. *Proceedings and Publications of the American Sociological Society. 20*, 40-46.

GAO Report, June 2008. Census Bureau Should Take Action to Improve the Credibility and Accuracy of Its Cost Estimate for the Decennial Census.

http://www.gao.gov/new.items/d08554.pdf

Rosenberg, Morris. 1989. Society and the Adolescent Self-Image. Revised edition. Middletown, CT: Wesleyan University Press.

Chapter 7

Designing a Study: Introduction to Writing a Research Paper

Creating an Introduction with a Literature Review

7.1 The Task of Writing

Writing a research paper is a difficult task for many students. It involves choosing a topic, taking in a lot of information by reading previous research, and asking a researchable question about that topic. Let's take this one part at a time. It might be useful for you to think through each section before going on to the next so you can stay focused on your goal. The first section involves choosing a topic: before you read ahead about the literature review and the research question, make sure you have a good topic in mind. This chapter is designed to give you a brief overview of this process. Going through the process of composing an APA style introduction is required for full understanding.

Keep in mind that although this chapter can give you information about writing a good research paper, each paper you read will teach you more. Look at the design of the introduction section of each paper you read. Keep in mind that you are doing quantitative research, so assess whether or not the authors are measuring something quantitatively, or are doing qualitative work.

The last part of this chapter will introduce APA format.

7.2 Choosing a Topic

Finding an appropriate topic is partly easy, and partly difficult. The first part is easy: think about your favorite topic in your major and answer the following questions. What interested you the most about that topic? Were there any unanswered questions about that topic? Think back to when you were learning about something that interested you. What did you find so interesting?

The topic has to be something you can work with and that will keep your interest. There are an infinite number of topics you could write a paper on and study. Narrowing down your general topic into something that is measurable can take time. If this is your first attempt, be careful not to over reach. It is okay to keep your topic and research plan simple. Make sure that you are addressing a specific topic and that you will be able to measure it in some way. Some topics might be difficult for you to quantitatively study: topics that involve children, prisoners, or groups of people you have no access to may be difficult to study. However, topics that involve opinions and information about the general population can be simple to study and yield good information. Consider a topic that involves comparing groups based on sex, race, age, or some specific behavior or belief system (i.e., gamers and non-gamers, democrats and republicans, Catholics and non-catholic Christians, athletes and non-athletes, etc. Comparing more than two groups is also okay.)

Make sure you have access to your groups: studying class differences is surely interesting, but make sure you have access to people in vastly different classes. (Often, your peers are in the same socioeconomic class as you.) This is not nearly a comprehensive list, but should give you an idea about what is possible.

Now that you have chosen a topic, review what you know about the topic, and make sure you can answer "yes" to the following questions:

"Do I care enough about the topic to spend time on it?"

"Am I going to be able to look at quantifiable differences between groups?"

"Do I have access to the groups I want to study?"

"What will I be measuring?"

For our purposes, it is also important to measure at least one construct using an index or a scale. We care about how people feel, and we care about abstract concepts. We are not interested in simple observations, like whether men or women drink more alcohol, as both of those variables can be measured with a single question, and there is no need to use an index or scale.

7.3 The Literature Review

[Finding appropriate material is its own topic. If you do not know how to use an article search tool, stop reading here and find a librarian to help you. You will need the skills to find and access scholarly journals.]

The literature review can serve a dual purpose. It is an experience for you to get well acquainted with your topic, and it eventually gives you material for part of your introduction. You may even find an article that answers your original research question. This is useful, because you may think of a better way to measure whatever the authors measured, or you may get a new idea about something you could measure. Often, a researcher who doubts another researchers results will try to replicate their study. When you are reading, take in as much information as you can. With each paper you read, ask:

"What is the author's hypothesis?"

"How did the author(s) test the hypothesis?"

"What are the variables?"

(Consider the way they conceptualize and operationalize their variables.)

"How did the data relate to the hypothesis?

There are, of course, many more questions you can ask, but being able to answer these questions will give you a good understanding of the research you are reading.

There are two main ways to go about doing a literature review. One way is to simply seek to answer a question. Often, students will be given an assignment to write about a topic, ranging from the function of the amygdala to the reasons behind the Libyan revolution. This is a simple literature review and requires no new ideas from the student. Another type of literature review is as a way to collect information to justify a hypothesis. The sources cited are used by the student in the development of a new idea. Published papers using quantitative research can provide numerous examples of this way of using past literature to come up with a new idea.

You will find many papers related to your topic. However, for many of the sources you find, you will read only the title of the paper before you decide it is not an appropriate source. For others, you might not get through the abstract before you find it does not address your topic the way you would like. The most useful papers are the ones that are so relevant to your topic you find yourself pouring through the methods section, trying to understand exactly what the researchers did.

As you read, keep track of the reference information so you can find the paper again or use it as a reference for your paper. This consists of the author's name(s), publication date, title of the article, title of the journal, and issue numbers and pages. (See the end of this chapter for an APA introduction.) You will collect similar information from books or book chapters. Avoid magazines and blogs, and anything that is not peer reviewed. They may give you ideas, but the information they contain can not be trusted. Even books are not as good as peer reviewed journals, because books can be published more easily than journal articles.

With each paper you read, you will be refining your topic. Think about how all of the papers you read fit together. Often, you can see a progression of research on the topic. You might want to start with broad articles about the topics, or what are called "review articles." Review articles summarize a lot of research on the topic and do a good job of describing the progression of research on that topic, but they often do not contain original research.

The literature you review in your introduction will show a logical progression. By the time you write your hypothesis, a reader should be able to guess what it is! Again, look at the papers you are reading, and let them be your guide as to how to introduce a topic and build to a hypothesis.

7.4 Asking a Question

Keep in mind that you are going to be doing a research project. Your project will be a survey, so you will have to ask a question that you can find the answer to with a survey. In "Choosing a Topic," it was suggested that you keep in mind that you would want to be comparing two groups. Composing a survey will be discussed later, but know that you will be able to measure things like opinions, behaviors, and preferences. These things can be measured by asking a series of questions.

Some things are easier to measure than others. People are generally happy to tell you about their likes and dislikes or about non-controversial behavior. Questions about sexual behavior and illegal activity, such as drug use, can often lead people to give incomplete or dishonest information. People are especially reticent if they are not completely sure that the information they are giving you is anonymous and confidential.

A good research question can seek to measure the differences between groups or the relationship between two variables. A good research question should be about something that is quantifiable and measurable, like opinions, behaviors, and preferences.

7.5 Putting It All Together

Once you have collected a series of articles on your topic and have collected enough background to write your introduction section, start writing your paper. Tell the reader why the topic is interesting, and use plenty of citations. Describing (in your own words) the work of others demonstrates your knowledge of the topic, and citing your sources protects you from *plagiarism*. Plagiarism in research means that you took an idea from someone else and did not give them credit for it. It can be as blatant as outright copying from another researcher, or as subtle, as basing an idea of your own on something an author suggested and not giving them credit. Plagiarism in research is considered scientific fraud and can mean the end of a career or a failing grade.

Continue to build up your topic until you reach your hypothesis. Your hypothesis should be clear and describe the relationship you expect to find between your variables or whatever it is you are studying.

Operationalizing your variables and describing how you will measure them will take place later, in your Methods section. Sections are divided up by the type of information they are expected to supply the reader.

A complete APA research paper contains the following sections:

Abstract
Introduction
Methods
Results
Discussion
References

A cover page is also included in APA format. For a project that involves writing an introduction, the only parts to write are the *introduction* section and the *reference* section. Each time you cite an author's work, you must include the reference for that work in the reference section.

Note: In coming up with your research question, you will consider the evidence you might find that would support or fail to support your hypothesis. Finding something statistically is much better than not finding something. While a *null result* (a finding that is not statistically significant) does not allow you to reject the null hypothesis, it does not necessarily support the null hypothesis. When you fail to find something, there are two possible explanations for your failure to find something. The first possible reason is that there really is no effect to be found. The second possible explanation is that you did something wrong in your research design. Perhaps the effect was small and your measure was imprecise, or perhaps your methods were invalid for what you wanted to measure. (The question in validity will be addressed later, but this basically means "were you actually measuring what you thought you were measuring.") Your research question can seem simple to you: don't be afraid of simplicity. Take the example of Latane & Bidwell (1977). Their research design was elegant in its simplicity, and provided good evidence for their hypothesis. They believed that females would show more affiliative behavior than males, and they operationalize affiliation as walking with other vs. walking alone. For data collection, all they had to do was count the number of males and females walking in groups or walking alone.

Note on Plagiarism:

It is actually quite easy to avoid plagiarism. Simply paraphrase everything you got from your sources during your literature review, and also cite where you got the material. Sometimes, people think they only have to use a citation if they quoted something. This is not true: every idea from another source must be cited. Quoting is not a very good idea anyway, as it often takes up space without being clear. If you paraphrase, it is far easier to build your argument.

When in doubt, cite your reference. If it is clear where an idea came from, you do not have to cite. Consider the following example:

People are more likely to vote A under condition B (Smith & Jones, 2012). The authors state that...

Since the second sentence begins with "The authors state that" it is clear that the idea from the first sentence is being continued, and does not need to be cited again. Section 7.7 will give examples of proper references, and where to find information on APA rules for paper writing.

7.6 Completing the Study

Once the research has been proposed, it must be carried out. The rest of the sections in an original research paper are Method, Results, and Discussion.

As was previously noted, the *Method* section is where variables are operationalized. Generally, the Method section has three subsections: Participants, Materials, and Procedure. The Participants section describes the group that you studied. It is important to describe any variables you are measuring, and any possible "3rd variables" that may affect your dependent variable. If you are comparing males to females, for instance, it is useful to denote how many are in each group, the mean age of each group, and any other important characteristics. The Materials section describes what exactly was used to collect data. If a survey was used, then the variables measured and ways that indexes were created are described. It is important to include enough information that someone else could recreate the study, while avoiding anything that might be irrelevant. The Procedure section also contains just enough information for another researcher to recreate the study. It is useful here to describe the type of sample used, and the way that each participant was measured. Describe any particular task that each participant had to perform.

The *Results* section is where the values you found for the test statistics are summarized. For instance, if the research question is that males and females perform differently on a task, a t-test may be used to show whether or not a difference was found between the two groups. Any "3rd variables" can also be measured in order to show that those variables are not responsible. Showing that age, for instance, is not a factor, may be important depending on the hypothesis and type of groups.

The *Discussion* section is where the results are described in a greater context. Information on how the results support or fail to support various theories is included here. Also, ways to improve the study and areas for future research should be mentioned.

Lastly, an *abstract* is a short summary of the research, usually between 150 and 250 words. Try to summarize each of the sections, Introduction, Methods, Results, and Discussion, using two sentences or less per section. It is not usually acceptable to include actual statistical calculations here.

7.7 APA Writing Introduction

The proper format for a research paper is a set of rules established by the American Psychological Association (APA).

For any questions about APA format, refer to the following website from the Purdue Online Writing Lab (OWL):

http://owl.english.purdue.edu/owl/resource/560/01/

(Angeli, et al., 2010).

Here is a sample basic citation for a single-author journal article from OWL:

Author, A. A., Author, B. B., & Author, C. C. (Year). Title of article. *Title of Periodical, volume number*(issue number), pages.

Harlow, H. F. (1983). Fundamentals for preparing psychology journal articles. *Journal of Comparative and Physiological Psychology, 55*, 893-896.

The Purdue Online Writing Lab is your resource for all things APA. A sample APA paper can be found here:

http://owl.english.purdue.edu/media/pdf/20090212013008_560.pdf

The example they give is a student review and not a research paper so it does not contain a Methods or Results section, but it does a good job of demonstrating the proper use of APA rules. APA is best learned through doing, so it can be helpful to write your introduction section and then fit it into APA format by following the directions on the website.

Key Terms:

Abstract

Introduction

Literature review

Methods

Null results

Reference

Results

Discussion

References

Angeli, E., Wagner, J., Lawrick, E., Moore, K., Anderson, M., Soderland, L., & Brizee, A. (2010, May 5). *General format.* Retrieved from http://owl.english.purdue.edu/owl/resource/560/01/

Latane, B. & Bidwell, L. (1977). Sex and Affiliation in College Cafeterias. *Personality and Social Psychology Bulletin. 3*(4) 571-574.

Chapter 8

Statistical Testing: Comparing Groups and Comparing Variables

Topics:

8.1 Overview

You have received an introduction to specific statistical tests in the chapters on Making Observations, The Experiment, and The Survey. The purpose of this chapter is to expand on that information and make each test make sense in a greater context. The ways of asking questions about variables can be summarized into two inclusive types of tests: Part 1. comparing two groups (to each other), and Part 2.

comparing two variables to each other. All of the following tests will fit into one (or both) of these categories of tests. Some tests will assess the difference between more than two groups, and some will compare more than two variables. However, the basis of statistical testing is really as simple as comparing two things, to either assess the difference or to characterize the relationship.

In advanced statistics classes you will find far more information about statistics. The information here will make you capable of performing the following statistical tests in order to analyze data. There will not be much information on the statistical theory associated with each test. Most importantly, a researcher should know how to use each test and when to use each test.

8.2 Tests Part 1: Comparing Two Groups

Means tests: differences between two samples

The *t-test* is the most widely used test. It is sometimes called a "student's t" because when W. S. Gosset published it, he was working for the Guinness brewery in Ireland and they did not want him to make it known that they were using statistical techniques (it was a business secret), so "Student" was Gosset's pseudonym. Had management at Guinness been more open, it would either be known as "Gosset's t", or possibly "the Guinness t," which would forever associate the t-test with

Guinness beer and be known as possibly the best use of science for marketing in history.

The t-test is so useful because it allows you to calculate the difference between two groups even if you do not know the characteristics of the population. Often, the population parameters are not known, so the population mean and standard deviation must be approximated from the sample. This is accomplished by using the t-distribution to calculate the size and likelihood of the difference between the two groups.

Compare the *z-distribution*, which is a representation of the normal population, to the t-*distribution*, which is an approximation of the normal distribution (Figure 8.1 a,b). Because the true population mean and standard deviation are not known, there is more area in the tails. Especially look at 3 and -3 standard deviations from the mean for both distributions. The z-distribution has very little area there. The t-distribution, however, has more. This extra area is there because the t-distribution has to account for error in the estimation of the population mean and standard deviation. This adjustment is what allows us to use the t-test: it is accounting for the unknown!

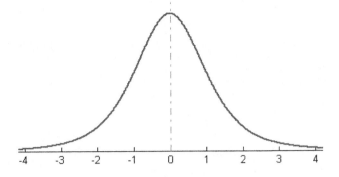

a. t-distribution, 4 degrees of freedom

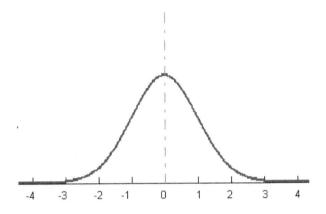

b. z-distribution ("normal" distribution)

Figure 8.1: The t-distribution and z-distribution. While similar, the major difference is the t-distribution has more area under the curve in the tails, while the area in the z-distribution is more centered on the mean, in this case, zero.

Another thing to note about these distributions is that most of the area is within 2-standard deviations of the mean. With normally distributed data, it is expected that most data will be close to the mean, and very little data will be further from the mean, with the probability getting smaller that the data come from the same distribution the further a point is from the mean.

For our purposes, there are two main types of t-tests: the paired samples t-test and the independent samples t-test. These relate to the idea of within subjects testing and between subjects testing. Within subjects testing is assessing the same group at two different times (i.e., before and after a stimulus) and is performed with the paired-samples t-test. Between subjects testing is used for assessing two different groups, and is performed with the independent-samples t-test.

Paired-Samples t-test

The *paired samples t-test* is the simplest test, and is similar to what is known as a "one sample t-test." The math behind it is so simple that it will be addressed here. Once you collect data from the same group tested twice, you calculate the mean and standard deviation of the difference between the before and after measures. Take the following example of scores on a math test given to four students on their first day of college and at the end of their Freshmen year. The research question is: "do students score higher on a math test after a year of college than they do on their first day?" The hypothesis would be "students score higher on a math test after their first year of college than they do on their first day."

First Day of College (FDC)	After Freshmen Year (AFY)	Difference (AFY-FDC)
60	85	25
75	97	22
55	73	18
48	80	32
		Mean=24.25
		SD=5.12

The idea is to compare the difference (AFY-FDC) scores from zero, which would mean 'no change.'

The t-score is calculated by the following:

t=	$\dfrac{\text{Mean Difference}}{\text{SD}/\sqrt{(n-1)}}$	$=\dfrac{24.25}{5.12/\sqrt{3}}$	=8.21

The t-value is 8.21, which is a very large t-value. To see how large, look at Figure 1a. 8.21 is the number of standard deviations from zero. Figure 1a only goes up to about four, and the area four standard deviations from zero is extremely small. Clearly, students do better on the test after a year of college. The associated p-value can be found in a lookup table or by using an online calculator. All that is needed to look up the score is to get the degrees of freedom, which is 3. Degrees of freedom in a paired-samples t-test are calculated by subtracting 1 from n (4-1=3).

It is simple to run the same test in IBM SPSS. Follow these steps:

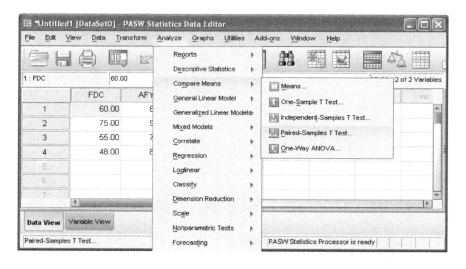

Select Analyze, Compare Means, Paired-Samples t test.

Next, put the two groups you want to compare into the boxes

marked "Variable 1" and "Variable 2" and then click the button marked

OK.

The output looks like this:

Paired Samples Test

| | | Paired Differences | | | | | | | |
| | | | | | 95% Confidence Interval of the Difference | | | | |
		Mean	Std. Deviation	Std. Error Mean	Lower	Upper	t	df	Sig. (2-tailed)
Pair 1	FDC - AFY	-24.25000	5.90903	2.95452	-33.65259	-14.84741	-8.208	3	.004

The most important boxes for now are t, df, and Sig. Note that the boxes are in a different location than they were for the independent-samples t-test.

The probability of getting results this extreme or more extreme, using a *two-tailed test*, is 0.004. However, a *one-tailed test* is used because directionality was predicted (it was predicted that AFY would be higher than FDC). A two-tailed test would be used if we said we think AFY and FDC would be different, but we did not know how. The p-value is the probability of finding results as extreme or more extreme than the t-value found in the null hypothesis test. Many statistical programs will give you the two-tailed p-value. In the case of the t-test, divide that two-tailed value by 2 because you are only looking in one tail, so you can ignore the probability that the results could be extreme in the other direction.

There is one other important step here. To make sure you are right, look at the direction of the sign. The difference in means is -24.25. This difference is calculated by subtracting the mean of AFY from the mean of FDC. Since AFY is expected to be bigger, then you expect a negative number. If you had a positive number, it would mean that the mean of FDC was higher than the mean of AFY. If you noticed this, you would not bother running a t-test because your prediction could not be true. If the mean of student scores was higher on their first day of college than it was after their first year, then no statistical test will lend support to your hypothesis!

Types of Errors: Type I and Type II

Since statistical tests are tests of the null hypothesis, there are two types of errors that can be made in interpreting results. A Type I error occurs when you reject the null, even if the null is true. This happens when a study is performed incorrectly, or by chance the data that a researcher collected happens to be an extreme sample. This does happen, and it can happen quite often. Experimental alpha is the amount of risk a researcher is willing to accept in making a Type I error. Often, researchers set alpha to 0.05. This means that there is a probability of finding data this extreme or more extreme *by chance* 5 times per 100 times the experiment is performed. Everything is probabilities. Nothing is ever proved.

A Type II error is when a researcher does not reject the null hypothesis, *even though the null is not true*. This can happen when the samples collected by a researcher are not statistically different, even though they come from different samples.

Table 1 shows you the possible interpretations for results, and when Type 1 and Type 2 errors occur.

	Results of Statistical Analysis (What you decide to believe)	
	No Difference	Difference
The Actual State of the World — No Difference	Correct rejection of experimental hypothesis	Type I Error
Difference	Type II Error	Correct rejection of the null hypothesis

Table 1: Possible outcomes of statistical analysis compared to the actual state of the world

Independent Samples t-test

The *independent samples t-test* is used for comparing two different groups. In order to calculate an independent samples t-value, the difference between group means must be calculated, and a value must be calculated for the standard deviation for each group. While these calculations are more complicated than the calculations for a paired samples t-test, a standard statistics package will easily calculate the t-value and p-value. These numbers are reported the same way the paired samples t-test information is reported.

Medians tests: differences between two samples

The t-test is simple, and it is often the best test to perform. However, it can lead to an increase in the chance of a type I or II error if you use it when you are not sure what the underlying distribution of the data looks like, or if the data are not interval-ratio data. The t-test is based on the idea that the data come from a normal distribution. The normal distribution (as in Figure 8.1 a,b) allows for the mean of each group to be used to calculate differences. Not all data, however, come from normal distributions. Consider housing prices and salaries: there are a number of extreme values that can throw off the mean (Figure 8.2). One extremely expensive home could alter the mean, but it can not be excluded as an outlier. In addition, ordinal data can not be analyzed using a t-test. Tests that rank-order data use the medians to calculate differences and are able to function when t-tests could not. Two median that will be discussed are analogous to the two t-tests discussed. The Wilcoxon sign-rank test can be used when a single group is tested twice, and the Mann-Whitney U test can be used when two separate groups are being compared. Both of these tests can be calculated easily using a standard statistical analysis package.

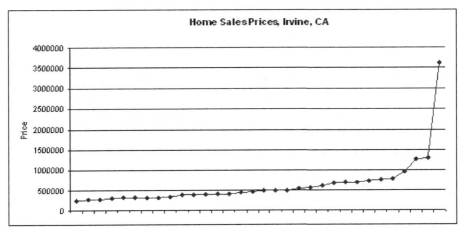

Figure 8.2: Sample of 32 homes sold in Irvine, CA, February to March 2011, ordered lowest price to highest price. The mean of these prices is 634,734, and the median is 473,500. Median is a better representation of what most people pay, rather than the mean.

Wilcoxon sign-rank test

The *Wilcoxon sign-rank test* is similar to the paired t-test, in that it is used to look at differences in scores from a single group that has been tested twice. In this case, the differences in scores are not used in the calculations themselves, but are ranked. Adding one observation to the example from earlier, the idea behind the Wilcoxon sign-rank test can be applied and understood.

(FDC)	(AFY)	(AFY-FDC)	Rank	Sign
60	85	25	4	+
75	97	22	3	+
55	73	18	2	+
48	80	32	5	+
68	62	-6	1	-

Two values are calculated: the sum of all positive values 4+3+2+5 (W_+=14) and the sum of all negative values (W_-=1). Then, knowing n, the associated p-value can be looked up in a table. The Wilcoxon sign-rank test is very simple to run in IBM SPSS. Notice that it looks very much like the paired-samples t-test! They are both tests that involve the same group of subjects, with each subject measured twice.

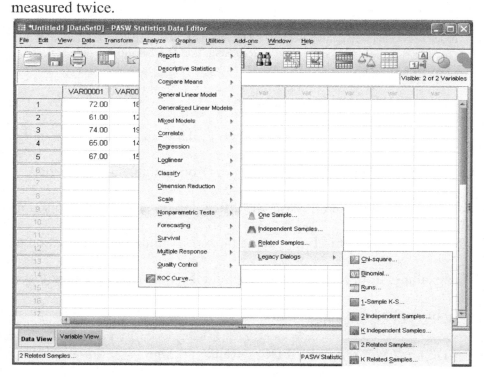

(*Reprint courtesy of International Business Machines Corporation, © SPSS.)

Select Analyze, Nonparametric Tests, Legacy Dialogs, and 2 Related Samples.

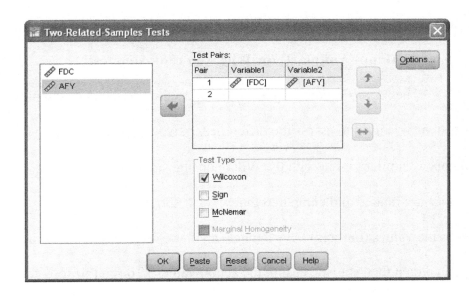

Next, put the two groups you want to compare into the boxes marked "Variable 1" and "Variable 2" and then click the button marked OK.

The output looks like this:

Test Statistics[b]

	AFY - FDC
Z	-1.826[a]
Asymp. Sig. (2-tailed)	.068

a. Based on negative ranks.

b. Wilcoxon Signed Ranks Test

SPSS converts the W to a z-score, and gives you the associated p-value (Asymp. Sig.)

(*Reprint courtesy of International Business Machines Corporation, © SPSS.)

Mann-Whitney U (or Wilcoxon rank-sum test)

The *Mann-Whitney U* test is similar to the independent samples t-test, as it is used to assess the difference in two different groups. The theory is similar to that with the Wilcoxon sign-rank test, in that the values are ranked and compared that way. It should be clear that extreme values (outliers) have a much smaller effect on statistics using ranked data than statistics using the actual values. To run this test, set up your data the same way you would for the independent-samples t-test. However, instead of selecting Analyze, Compare Means, and Independent-Samples T Test, in IBM SPSS select "Analyze, Non Parametric Tests, Legacy Dialogs, and 2 Independent Samples." The rest of the procedure is the same as for the independent-samples t-test.

8.3 Tests Part 2: Comparing Two Variables

Correlation: Relationships between two variables

Often, it is the relationship between variables that must be assessed, such as the relationship between height and weight, or the relationship between self-esteem and income. The question involved here is not about which is larger; that is irrelevant. The important question is about how a change in one variable affects the other. For instance, as height increases, is it true that weight usually increases? Do people who make more money have higher self-esteem? The answer to these questions can be found by computing a *correlation*. Correlation tells us how strongly one variable is predicted by the other. For instance, if I know someone's weight, how well can I guess their height?

Pearson's r

Pearson's r is the standard calculation for correlation. The purpose of the r statistic is to calculate the strength of the relationship between two variables. Take the following data on heights and weights:

Height (inches)	Weight (pounds)
72	182
61	125
74	190
65	145
67	150

Drawing the data in a *scatterplot* can often make it easier to understand. When the relationship between two variables is being assessed, one variable is the x-axis and the other is the y-axis. Arbitrarily in Figure 3, height is on the x-axis and weight is on the y-axis.

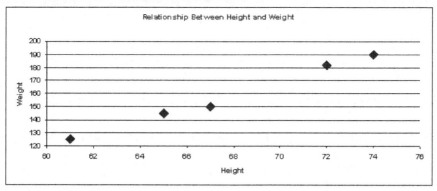

Figure 8.3: The relationship between Height and Weight: note the
observations with lower height also tend to have lower weight.

The relationship highlighted in Figure 8.3 is a *positive*

relationship because as height increases, so does weight. In a *negative*

relationship, as one value increases, the other value decreases. For

instance, as age increases, it is possible that physical activity decreases,

leading to a negative relationship between the variables "age" and

"physical activity."

The formula for correlation allows for a value between 0 and 1

to be calculated. 0 means that there is no correlation, and 1 means that

there is a perfect correlation, that all values form a perfect line. A

negative correlation, such as -1, is also a perfect correlation, it just

means that as one variable increases, the other decreases as in a

negative relationship. A correlation between -.4 and .4 is generally

considered to be very small. Note that different textbooks use different

scales for what is considered large and small in correlation coefficients.

-.4 to -.6	Small	.4 to .6
-.6 to -.8	Medium	.6 to .8
-.8 to -1	Large	.8 to 1

The formula is: $r = \dfrac{n\Sigma XY - (\Sigma X)(\Sigma Y)}{\sqrt{[n\Sigma X^2 - (\Sigma X)^2][n\Sigma Y^2 - (\Sigma Y)^2]}}$

Table 2: Calculations in performing correlation.

Height X	Height^2 X^2	Weight Y	Weight^2 Y^2	Weight*Height X*Y
72	5184	182	33124	13104
61	3721	125	15625	7625
74	5476	190	36100	14060
65	4225	145	21025	9425
67	4489	150	22500	10050
ΣX=339	ΣX^2=23095	ΣY=792	ΣY^2=128374	ΣXY=54264

All the numbers needed to calculate the correlation are in Table 2. The correlation calculated using the above data is 0.996. This is an extremely strong correlation, as it is very close to 1. The correlation between height and weight is probably not this strong, but the correlation in the data here is. This is a small sample, and small samples can not often be trusted to represent the general population. Pearson's r is reported as: r(4)=0.996. The p-value is not extremely important with correlations, as the size of the correlation is the important piece of information.

Kendall's tau

Kendall's tau is calculated by ranking the size of each observation for each variable separately, and then calculating how many times two values next to each other must be exchanged in order to make the first variable look like the second variable.

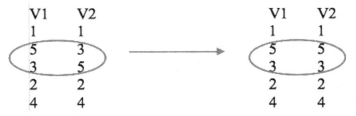

Now V1 and V2 look alike, so there is no "distance" between them. This was accomplished by switching only two values one time in V2 to make it look like V1. Tau does not require the data to be normally distributed, nor does it require interval/ratio data. Tau also has a value between 0 and 1, with a – sign denoting a negative relationship. Tau is reported similarly to r.

It takes just a few steps to calculate both Pearson's r and Kendall's tau in SPSS. In fact, you can calculate both of them at the same time.

Once you input the data, select Analyze, Correlate, and Bivariate.

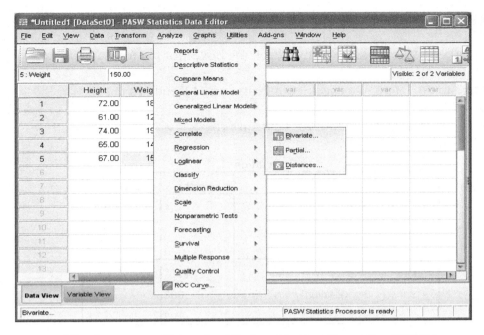

(*Reprint courtesy of International Business Machines Corporation, © SPSS.)

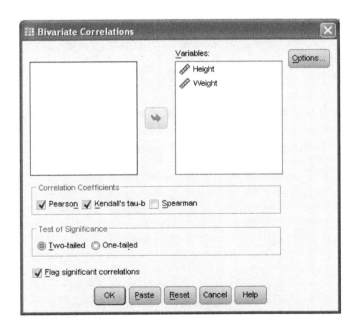

(*Reprint courtesy of International Business Machines Corporation, © SPSS.)

Next, place the variables you want to correlate into the box marked "Variables." Finally, check the boxes for the tests you would like to do. Here, we check both Pearson and Kendall's tau-b.

Here is the output for Pearson's r:

Correlations

		Height	Weight
Height	Pearson Correlation	1	.996**
	Sig. (2-tailed)		.000
	N	5	5
Weight	Pearson Correlation	.996**	1
	Sig. (2-tailed)	.000	
	N	5	5

**. Correlation is significant at the 0.01 level (2-tailed).

Note that the correlation is .996, and the Sig. (p-value) is reported as .000. (Remember that you would report it as p<.001.)

Here is the output for Kendall's tau:

Correlations

			Height	Weight
Kendall's tau_b	Height	Correlation Coefficient	1.000	1.000*
		Sig. (2-tailed)	.	.
		N	5	5
	Weight	Correlation Coefficient	1.000**	1.000
		Sig. (2-tailed)	.	.
		N	5	5

*. Correlation is significant at the 0.05 level (2-tailed).

**. Correlation is significant at the 0.01 level (2-tailed).

Note that Kendall's tau reports the correlation value as 1. This is an odd result: it means there is a perfect correlation in the data. If you look back to the dataset, however, it becomes clear. The top value for height is matched with the top value for weight. The second value for height, is matched with the second value for weight. If you consider what Kendall's tau is calculating, it is merely how the rank-order of the first variable matches up with the rank-order of the second variable. When you look at the data, you can see this is the case! You will also note that no Sig. (p-value) is reported. This is because if the correlation is perfect (=+1 or -1) then the probability of this results being produced by chance is infinitely small.

The issue leads us to ask two important questions.

1. Is the sample size sufficient to get a good estimate?

2. Is the data a random sample of the population?

We must answer yes to both questions if we are to be able to trust our data. In this case, we can answer yes to neither of the questions. The sample size of 5 is much too small for a good estimate, and we do not know the origin of the data. If you would like to get an idea of the actual population-wide correlation between height and weight, we must improve our sample and our sample size.

8.4 Using the Right Test at the Right Time

Knowing the correct test to do can depend on a lot of factors. This is the most challenging of all the concepts in statistical testing. In the real world there will not be signs saying "do a t-test here!" or "this requires a correlation!" A researcher is required to understand what kind of test to do. Fortunately, this can be simplified!

Start with the following question: "Is there a relationship between height and weight?"

The first step is to *identify the variables you would like to assess*. In this case, they are 'height' and 'weight'. Next, identify the kinds of variables they are: nominal, ordinal, interval, or ratio. (These categories are described in Chapter 4.) The variable 'height' is on a ratio scale because it is a measure that has a true zero, and the distance between each measure is consistent: the distance between one and two inches is the same as the distance between two and three inches, and so on. "Weight" is like height, so these are both ratio variables.

Table 3 below shows which test to use for analyzing various variable relationships. Once you decide what kind of analysis to do in your study, all you have to do is look at the table to determine the appropriate statistical test.

Table 3: Variables and Associated tests

Variable types		Test
2 interval/ratio	-	correlation (r)
2 ordinal	-	correlation (tau)
2 nominal	-	χ^2
1 nominal 1 interval/ratio	2 different groups	Independent samples t-test
1 nominal 1 interval/ratio	Same group 2 times	Paired-samples t-test
1 nominal 1 ordinal	2 different groups	Mann-Whitney U
1 nominal 1 ordinal	Same group 2 times	Wilcoxon sign-rank

These basic tests will allow you to analyze all kinds of data. Once you can identify your variables and the researcher question, then knowing which test to perform is simple. There are any far more complicated tests and analyses, but they can usually be reduced to one of these tests.

8.5 Graphing Data

This last section is on presenting your data. Graphing data, however, is a useful tool that goes beyond presentation. For instance, many researchers will be able to look at your graphs and be able to understand immediately whether or not a relationship exists in your data, before they even see the results of your statistical tests. Consider Figure 3 presented earlier in this chapter. You should have been able to look at that scatterplot and see immediately that as weight increases, so does height. No statistical test was necessary for you to see the relationship. Sometimes relationships are less clear, and sometimes they are more complex.

This next section will present instructions for creating scatterplots and bar-graphs. You will be guided though the process by the use of step-by-step instructions for using a free online tool called calc from Libre Office. It is similar to other office suites you may be familiar with, but it is an open-source program ideal for use here because anyone can download and run it for free. If you know how to use another program, please feel free to do so. Just look at the images and create graphs similar to those shown here.

The Scatter-plot

The Scatter-plot is used when you have two variables and you want to see the relationship between them. If your statistical test is a correlation, then the scatter-plot is the best way to present your data. Each of your subjects gives you two pieces of data, and you place those side by side in your Calc spreadsheet.

For instance, you have two measures for each subject, one where you give them a score on a measure of functionality and another where you give them a score on awareness. The data should be organized like this:

Next, select both columns, including the column titles. Notice how both columns are tinted blue. Notice the buttons on the toolbar, particularly the one that looks like a graph. It is circled above. Once you push that button you get a screen with options for you to choose the graph you want.

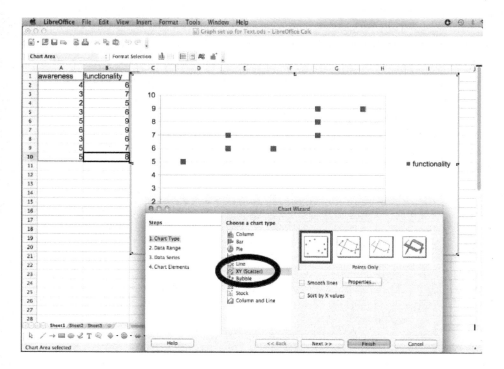

In the dialog box that asks you what type of chart you want,

select the one that says XY (Scatter). It is circled above. Click on the

button that says Next >> until you see a screen that looks like this:

Here you have the option to title your scatter-plot and label the X and Y axes. Click finish, and you're almost done. One the graph, you will see that the label for one of your columns is now on the right, showing you what the blue boxes represent. However, this information is redundant and should be deleted. It is easy to make changes to these graphs. Just click on the box (here it says "functionality") and press the delete button.

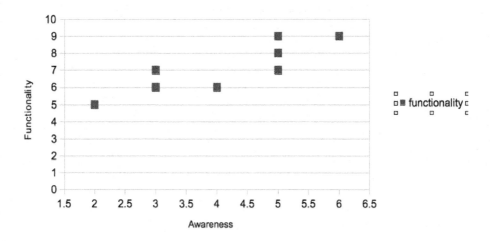

Relationship Between Awareness and Functionality

Now you have only one more step. The plot could look better:
for instance, in your data for the variable awareness you only have
whole numbers, but on the X-axis you have half values. Double click
on the axis, and a dialog box like this will appear.

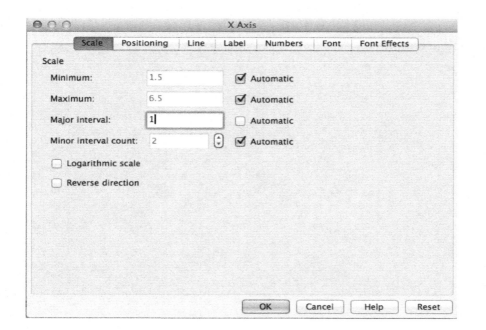

You can change the "Major interval" to 1, so you no longer have those half-ticks on the plot. Now your plot looks like this:

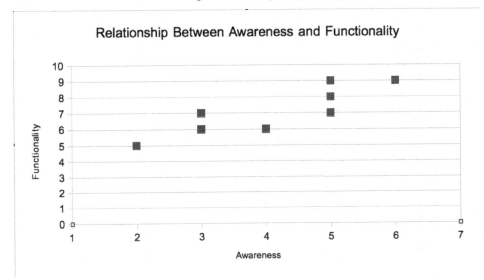

If you like, you can even delete the values on the Y-axis so that it only runs from 4-10. Empty space is rarely useful to show.

Bar Graph

The last type of plot we will examine is called the "Bar Graph", or sometimes the "Column Graph." The steps in the production of this kind of plot are more involved, but will be carefully explained here. Be sure to follow each step as directed. To begin, set up your data like this:

F16

	A	B	C	D	E	F	
1	sex	score					
2	female	3					
3	female	4					
4	female	6					
5	female	2					
6	female	3					
7	female	2					
8	female	2					
9	female	6					
10	female	5					
11	female	4					
12	female	6		male	female		
13	female	3				mean	
14	male	2				stdev	
15	male	3				se	
16	male	3					
17	male	4					
18	male	3					
19	male	4					
20	male	2					
21	male	2					
22	male	4					
23	male	3					
24	male	5					
25							

Notice that you have two variables: one tells you which group a subject belongs to, and the other tells you the score that subject received. This is not enough, however, to create the graph. You must perform some calculations first. It will help to create a new table in another part of the spreadsheet, where you label two columns "male" and "female," and three rows "mean," "stdev," and "se." You will be calculating those three values for both of your groups. Often, a statistical package will calculate those things for you, but here we will

use the functions included in Calc. There are other ways to do these

things, but these instructions will use the simplest way.

	A	B	C	D	E	F
1	sex	score				
2	female	3				
3	female	4				
4	female	6				
5	female	2				
6	female	3				
7	female	2				
8	female	2				
9	female	6				
10	female	5				
11	female	4				
12	female	6		male	female	
13	female	3	11 R x 1 C	=average(B14:B24)		mean
14	male	2				stdev
15	male	3				se
16	male	3				
17	male	4				
18	male	3				
19	male	4				
20	male	2				
21	male	2				
22	male	4				
23	male	3				
24	male	5				
25						

If you like, input the data as shown here so you can see how this

works on your own. In the empty box below "male," type

"=average(B14:B24)" and press enter. Now do the same thing below the box labeled "female." You'll notice, however, than instaed of

typing (B14:B24) you will have to type (B2:B13).

LibreOffice File Edit View Insert Format Tools Data Window Help

Graphs for textbook 2.ods – LibreO

Arial   10   B I U

AVERAGE   =average(B2:B13)

	A	B	C	D	E	F
1	sex	score	12 R x 1 C			
2	female	3				
3	female	4				
4	female	6				
5	female	2				
6	female	3				
7	female	2				
8	female	2				
9	female	6				
10	female	5				
11	female	4				
12	female	6		male	female	
13	female	3		3.181818182	=average(B2:B13)	
14	male	2				stdev
15	male	3				se
16	male	3				
17	male	4				
18	male	3				
19	male	4				
20	male	2				
21	male	2				
22	male	4				
23	male	3				
24	male	5				
25						

Now to the box under "male" in the row that says "stdev." Type "=stdev(B14:B24)" and press enter.

	LibreOffice	File	Edit	View	Insert	Format	Tools	Data	Window	Help

Graphs for textbook 2.ods – LibreO

Arial   10   B I U

AVERAGE   fx ✖ ✓   =stdev(B14:B24)

	A	B	C	D	E	F
1	sex	score				
2	female	3				
3	female	4				
4	female	6				
5	female	2				
6	female	3				
7	female	2				
8	female	2				
9	female	6				
10	female	5				
11	female	4				
12	female	6		male	female	
13	female	3		3.181818182	3.833333333	mean
14	male	2		=stdev(B14:B24)		stdev
15	male	3				se
16	male	3				
17	male	4				
18	male	3				
19	male	4				
20	male	2				
21	male	2				
22	male	4				
23	male	3				
24	male	5				
25						

In the next box under "female," type "=stdev(B2:B13)" and press enter, and now you have calculated both the means and standard deviations for both groups. Next, you will calculate the standard errors.

The standard error is an important calculation here because we want to use error bars. Error bars make graphs useful. Under "male" in the "se" column, type the following:

male	female	
3.181818182	3.833333333	mean
0.981649817	1.585922922	stdev
=D14/SQRT(11)		se

Here, you are dividing the standard deviation by the square root of the number of observations (n) for each group. Since there are 11 male subjects, you will divide .982 by the square root of 11 (about 3.3) and this will give you the standard error. Standard error is the reason that as your n increases, your precision also increases. This means that usually, the more subjects you have, the more likely you are to find a significant difference because your standard error increases. You can see this, by dividing 9.82 by the square root of 11, and then increase the n. Try dividing by the square root of 25, then 100, and then 400. Notice that your standard error decreases each time!

Do the same calculations for "se" for "female," and you are ready for the next step. Notice that your n for the "female" group is 12. The n does not have to be exactly the same when comparing two groups, but it is good to keep it close.

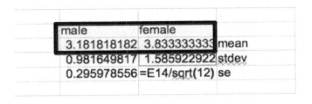

male	female	
3.181818182	3.833333333	mean
0.981649817	1.585922922	stdev
0.295978556	=E14/sqrt(12)	se

Now, select only four boxes in the little table you made: male and female, and the box under each.

Click on the icon on the toolbar that looks like a graph. This is the same icon you clicked on to create the scatter-plot.

And you will see a dialog box that looks like this.

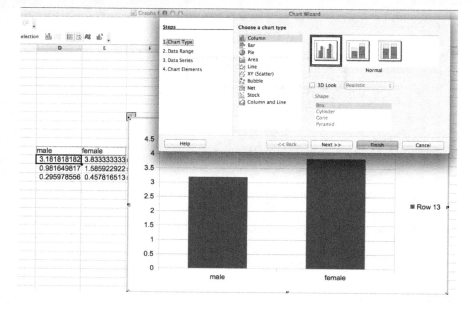

Since "Column" is the default selection under "chart type," click on the button that reads: "Next >>" until you see a dialog box that allows you to label chart elements.

Now you can title the graph and label the axes however you like.

When you are finished making your choices, click the button that reads "Finish" and you will see a graph that looks like this:

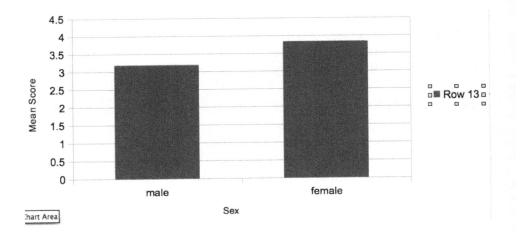

First, click on the box on the right that reads "Row 13" (graphs you create will probably have a different label here. It does not matter: it is meaningless unless you are making a large number of comparisons.) Once you click on this box and you see the six green boxes around it, as above, press delete and it will disappear.

Back to error bars: we ignored those calculations at first, but now it is time to consider them. When you look at the two columns comparing the scores for "male" and "female," you see that the box for female is taller. Does this mean that females have a higher score than males? Many people will say "yes," but this is not necessarily true. You can not tell for sure without error bars. Consider what this means. Error bars tell you how much variability there is between individuals within each group. All you are plotting here, however, is the mean. A t-test, for instance, uses both information about the mean and information about the standard error in order to decide if there is a significant difference between the groups. An experienced researcher can look at a graph with error bars and immediately tell whether there is a difference between the groups. If there are no error bars, there is no real information in the graph.

Right click on either of the boxes. You will see the following options:

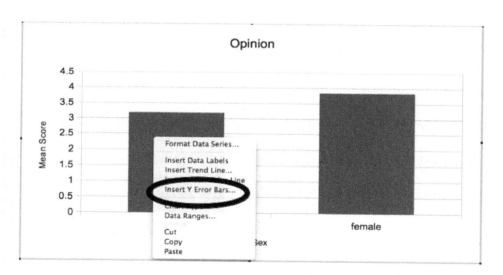

Select "Insert Y Error Bars." A dialog box will come up that looks like this:

Error Bars for Data Series 'Row 13'

Y Error Bars | Line

Error Category

- ○ Constant Value
- ○ Percentage
- ○ Standard Deviation ⬍
- ● Cell Range

Error Indicator

- ● Positive and Negative
- ○ Positive
- ○ Negative

Parameters

Positive (+) `$Sheet1.$D$15:$E$15`

Negative (–) `$Sheet1.$D$15:$E$15`

☐ Same value for both

OK | Cancel | Help | Reset

Pay careful attention to the writing where it says "Parameters." You will input the values you like in exactly the format used here. Also note that the value is the same for both positive and negative error bars. "$Sheet1.$D$15:$E$15" tells Calc to insert error bars that have the value found in boxes D15 and E15 in Sheet1. Remember that you calculated those values, and the value for "males" and "females" differs. Be careful not to use the values for standard deviation (stdev), only the values for standard error (se) for both the positive and negative values. When you are finished, you will have a graph that looks like this:

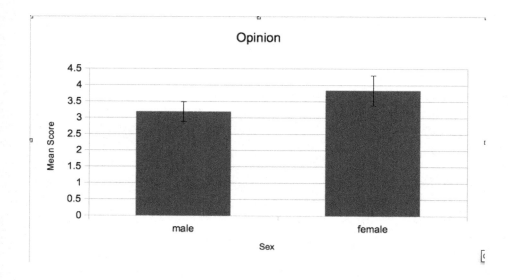

This is a very nice plot, and we will make only one more

change. Notice the values on the left on the Y-axis. Like we saw in the

scatter-plot, these include half-numbers, even though we only have

whole numbers in the data. We want to change the scaling of this axis.

Double click the axis, and this will come up:

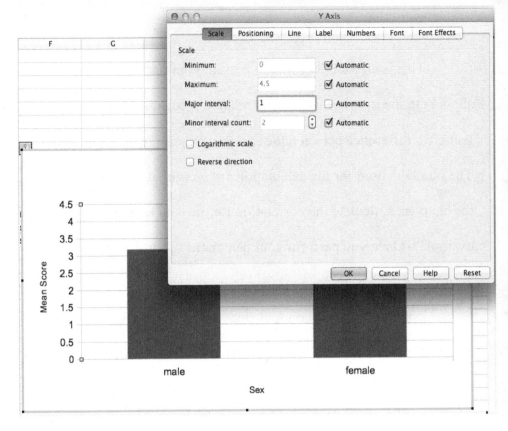

Change the "Major interval" from .5 to 1, and you are finished.

Click "OK," and your graph now looks like this:

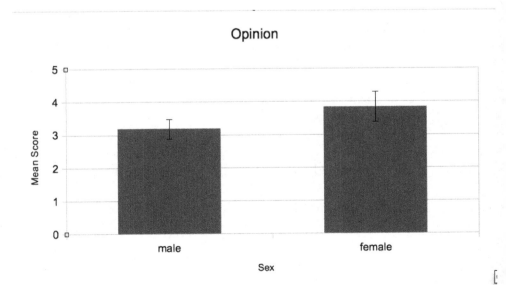

Opinion

This is an excellent way to present your data. Your columns show both the mean as well as the relative precision of that calculation. Is there a difference between the two groups presented in this graph? The numbers used for the calculation are presented in a table earlier in the chapter. Calculate the correlation for the data used in the scatterplot example? Once you perform your calculations, scroll past the "Key Terms" for the answer.

That is all we are going to study here. You have seen three different types of studies, from the planning stage through the analysis and presentation of data. Enjoy designing your own projects!

Key Terms:

Bar Graph

Column Graph

Correlation

independent samples t-test

Kendall's tau

Mann-Whitney U

Negative relationship

one-tailed test

paired samples t-test

Pearson's r

Positive relationship

t-distribution

t-test

two-tailed test

Type I error

Type II error

Scatterplot

Wilcoxon sign-rank

z-distribution

Answers:

Bar Graph example: There is no statistical difference between the two groups on this measure. (p>.05)

Scatter-plot example: There is a strong correlation between the variables.

Postscript

This text has been a simplified introduction. Many related concepts were left out. For instance, a colleague of mine argued that I could have discussed the central limit theorem in talking about p-value. I agree that the CLT is an important concept, but my goal here has been to only address ideas that are central to students being able to design, analyze, and interpret one's own research project. Too much information can obfuscate the central goal.

I added the instructions for making graphs at the end, as I believe being able to present information simply is important.

If you have any suggestions, please contact me at benjaminalexandermis@gmail.com. Please know that I will gladly consider any suggestions that will enhance the goal of this text.

Thank you,

Benjamin A. Mis

Acknowledgments

I would like to thank Frederick Mis for his useful notes on several topics and Nancy Mis for help with language and clarity. Special thanks to Jose Tabares and Maritza Leon who took the time to read though prior drafts and set me on the right track.

Thank to Carole Campbell for giving me the opportunity to teach Quantitative Research methods many times, and to Lily Monji and Jackie Southern for helping with so many scheduling and planning issues.

Thank you to Amy Bradley and IBM for arranging permission to reprint screenshots from SPSS.

Special thanks to all the developers of Calc, the spreadsheet tool in the open-source Libre Office suite.

I am, of course, indebted to the students I have had the pleasure of teaching. You have taught me what you need to know, and inspired me to put together this introduction to better help you understand the topic and succeed at research.

Made in the USA
Middletown, DE
24 August 2019